Experiencing God's Love Through Israel

Experiencing God's Love Through Israel

A Pictorial Devotional

Anne Richardson

A.M. Richardson Publishing
San Diego, California 92124

www.amrichardsonpublishing.com
www.annemarierichardson.com

Book Cover design by Chou Hallegra – graceandhopeconsulting.com

ISBN: 978-1-7329544-6-5

Introduction

Are you longing for something new, something that will nourish your soul and draw you closer to the heart of God?

And what if you could travel to Israel right now? No threat from a pandemic. You wouldn't have to go through security lines at the airport or social distance on a plane. All you need is a small carry-on bag with a few essentials. All this with the safety and comfort of home. And the cost? Just what you paid for this book. What a deal!

And best of all, your traveling companion is someone who loves you more than anyone else. Someone who wants what is best for you, has your back, and longs to draw you closer in relationship. His name is El Shaddai. Or in English: God.

This is not your typical devotional book, Bible study, or tour guidebook filled with details. Instead, this book's design is more like a pilgrimage, which is defined as a journey in search of new or expanded meaning of self, others, and God through the experience. The focus is on gleaning spiritual insights of the places, not so much on obtaining information. The hope is that the pilgrimage will lead to a transformation from God after one has returned home to everyday life. This is what happened to me. My hope is this will happen for you.

There are 60 days of devotions, each containing at least one photo. Most are my personal photos, and a few are from my friends. You will see both sacred sites and some of everyday life in Israel. I will share a little bit about the photo, and I encourage you to google the site if you desire to learn more information.

The days are not dated. Although my pilgrimage was two weeks, you get to decide how many days and weeks your journey will take. A suggested spiritual practice or exercise will be provided for you to engage in each day; however, you get to decide what spiritual practice, prayer, or scripture to reflect on. The purpose is to deepen your relationship with God and discover what he is inviting you into.

John Calvin (1509-1564)[1] was a famous French theologian and pastor during the protestant reformation. He stated, "To know God is to know thyself, and to know thyself is to know God." The spiritual practices in this book are *tools* that foster self-awareness, drawing one into a deeper relationship with God. I use the analogy of a broken shoulder. You can go to the doctor and learn all about his or her degrees, licenses, and expertise. You can also learn more about the shoulder, how it is created and how it works. However, in order for you to experience full function and mobility of the shoulder, you need to spend time with the Physical Therapist and do the daily exercises in your home. In the same way, a study of the Scriptures enriches and provides the groundwork we need and helps us get to know more about God. Yet spending time alone with him, being vulnerable, authentic, and self-aware, is what draws us into a deeper relationship with God. Most people settle for a shoulder that can move the arm up and down, so to speak. But you can have a shoulder like a trapeze artist that always allows you to soar through the sky!

Although my faith is Christian, I welcome any of you who want to take this journey. Even though most of the spiritual practices in this book are based on the Christian faith, many are beneficial for people of all faiths. My tour guide was Jewish, with a strong belief in God and tremendous knowledge about the area and the history. He said that Jesus did great things for the people, but he didn't believe he was divine. We enjoyed our time together, respecting each other's faiths.

"What was it like to go to Israel?" I am often asked. "It was one of my favorite pilgrimages ever!" I was grateful to do a private tour with my husband and our two adult daughters. I did not want another whirlwind all-day-tour-hit the ground running and listening to details, only to be left feeling exhausted at the end of each day. I wanted to go slow, to have time for quiet and reflection. For in being still is where I experience God.

"Be still and know I am God" Ps. 46:10

Having been a Christ follower all of my life, words can't express what it felt like to be where Jesus had walked. Now when I read the stories in the Bible, they come alive as I can imagine the scene where it took place. Although much has changed in 2,000 years, many ruins are still being discovered and excavated today. As I stood awestruck, in some places where historical stories from the Scriptures actually happened, my faith deepened.

I went on this pilgrimage, searching and longing to experience more of God. He blessed my desire by clearing the crowds for us, so we could have some space and quiet. My guide kept saying he couldn't believe it because these places are usually packed with busloads of people. With a heart full of gratitude and a smile on my face, I said to myself: *"Thank you, God. I love you, too."*

Now, as I write this book, we are dealing with the effects of COVID19, a virus that has shaken the world. For those of you who may not be able to travel to Israel, I invite you now to travel with me, through your imagination, with the help of the pictures and devotions in this book. Feel free to go at your own pace. You may wish to move through each day or stop and pause, stretching a day's spiritual practice into a week. Some of the day's practices will speak more to you than others, and that is okay. Go...stay... be with God, however long you need. Or feel free to take a *Shabbat* or Sabbath: day of rest. Most of all, I hope you will deepen your relationship with God as together, we wander through the places of this ancient Holy place, exploring the treasured sites of Israel.

Getting Ready

Grab your Bible, pen, a journal, some water, comfy clothes and come along with me. Find a place, a space that is quiet, preferably in your home, where you can be alone with God. Leave the cell phone and computer behind. Turn off any outside (or inside) noise if you can. Be open to whatever the day may bring or for whatever experience you may have. Let go of any unrealistic expectations. You may not feel or experience anything from God on a certain day, or you may receive insight from him later, and that is normal. Know he is with you always, like the air we breathe, whether you feel his presence or not.

Each day, there is a photo with a brief description and spiritual practice or exercise. These practices are *tools* that allow God to draw you closer to him. Some practices might take longer than a day. Even though I visited several sites in one day, I broke it down, so you can *take your time*. Stretch the day out to as many days as you need. As I mentioned previously, I will share a little bit about the photo, but you are welcome to Google it for more detailed information about the site.

Often, a spiritual practice involves being quiet or contemplative. This is not about emptying the mind but learning how to put aside all those thoughts spinning around in our head and listen to God's gentle whisper (1Kings 19: 11-12). I talk more about the benefit of silence and solitude in Day One.

I have chosen five spiritual practices or exercises, which have been around for a long time: Visio Divina, Reflection, Prayer, Imaginative Prayer, and Journaling. The pondering questions are developed from my years of being a spiritual director. These practices will help you experience more of God's presence and gain insight or self-awareness of your desires and needs. You can pick one or more of these five practices to do each day or decide to do the practice(s) I suggest each day. Or you may incorporate one of your favorite practices or spiritual disciplines that help you connect with God.

> *"Are you tired? Worn out? Burned out on religion? Come to me. Get away with me and you will recover your life. I will show you how to take a real rest."*
> Matthew 11: 28 MSG.

Visio Divina or Divine Visual (Reflecting Through Art or Photography)

- Spend several minutes gazing at the photo of the day before reading the text.

- What do you notice?

- What jumps out at you?

- What is God saying to you through this picture?

- After you read the devotion, go back to the photo and spend a few minutes. Allow God to speak to you through the photo.

Reflection

- Whether it is reflection on scripture or the questions, the purpose is to search deeper within your heart, mind, and soul for what this means to you or what God is inviting you into.

- Spend some time reflecting on the questions presented to some of the practices. Ask God for wisdom.

- When reflecting on scripture, **slowly** read the scripture verse or passage several times. Notice the phrases that you are most drawn to.

- Ask God for wisdom and insight with: What did this passage/story mean at the time, and What is God saying to me today?

- After the third reading, ask God what he is inviting you into, or to take action?

Prayer

- On certain days, I will suggest some prayers. Or you may choose your own prayers.

- Prayer is a conversation with God. Try to talk to him like you would a friend.

Imaginative Prayer

St. Ignatius of Loyola (1491-1556)[2] taught on using our imaginations in prayer. This is simply putting oneself in the scripture passage, either as an observer or one of the characters, and then allowing God to speak to you. Try for at least 15 minutes, as it takes time to really hear from God. This is one of my favorites!

- Sit quietly. Get comfortable in your chair. **Slowly** read the passage several times, allowing the scripture to move deeply into your heart. Now close your eyes. *If silence triggers any PTSD, then please refrain. Instead, try this practice with your eyes open and look at the picture.* Breathe deeply for a few minutes, focusing on each breath.

- Put yourself in the passage. Perhaps you are an observer or one of the characters.

- Use your senses. What do you see? What do you hear? Can you touch anything? What do you smell? Take some time imagining this scene.

- What do the characters look like? What is their body language like?

- Spend some time in this story, slowly going through each part.

- What is God saying to you through this passage?

- What is God inviting you to?

- What is your response to God?

- When you are ready, focus on your breathing. Feel your body in the chair. Then slowly open your eyes.

Journal

I strongly encourage you to journal your responses to the reflection questions, spiritual practices, or any experience you may have. Journaling is a powerful spiritual discipline which helps us gather our thoughts and feelings that are spinning in our heads, summarizing what is necessary, and making it clear by writing it down. You don't have to write an essay, just what you are learning, sensing, or being invited into by God.

Again, go at your own pace. You don't need to rush through this journey. Stay as long as you need. God may have something to say to you over a few days. And if one day does not speak to you, then feel the freedom to move on. You will benefit more from taking this slowly. One thing COVID19 taught me and others I know are: Slow down. Simplify. Let go of the busy, hurried life and *Be still*.

Making this a longer trip won't cost you any more money, but the experiences with God are *priceless*.

- What are you hoping for on this journey?
- What are your desires?

  Don't edit or judge your desires or try to write something super spiritual. Just be you. Be real. Write in your journal what your heart truly desires right now.

Dear Pilgrim
Dear Guide

This Sanctuary
is a House of Prayer and Silence.

Please give the explanation
outside the Church.

Thank You.

OPEN

Monday - Friday
8:00 - 17:00

Saturday
8:00 - 15:00

Sunday
CLOSED

open only for the Holy Mass

Day One
Silence

The Lord said (to Elijah), "Go out and stand on the mountain in the presence of the Lord, for the Lord is about to pass by." Then a great and powerful wind tore the mountains apart and shattered the rocks before the Lord, but the Lord was not in the wind. After the wind there was an earthquake, but the Lord was not in the earthquake. After the earthquake came a fire, the Lord was not in the fire. And after the fire came a gentle whisper.
1 Kings 19:11-12

There are great benefits in practicing silence and solitude as a part of this journey. As I previously mentioned, this is not about emptying your mind but learning how to put that spinning chatter in your head on pause. Being contemplative helps us release our control and be open to receive what God has for us. You will be able to hear God's gentle whisper when you are quiet. Also, solitude is not about loneliness, as you are never alone. Your traveling guide (The Holy Spirit) is with you always.

Jesus is our role model. He spent 40 days of silence and solitude in the desert before he started his ministry. He often retreated to a solitary place to pray. Yes, he served people and had an active ministry. But he also took time out to be alone and to listen to God. Jesus' service to others flowed out of the loving relationship he had with the Father.

Slow down, be still, and take some time to listen. This can be hard to do at first, but over time, it gets easier. Great insight and wisdom come to me when I am reflective in the quiet. Treat this time as a sanctuary of silence for your soul.

Spiritual Exercise: Being Silent

- Get comfortable in your chair. Feet on the floor. Arms on your lap with palms up. Close your eyes. Slowly, breathe in the cleansing breath of God, breathe out any distractions. Try this for a few minutes. If you are comfortable, imagine sinking into God's love as you sink into your chair.

- Notice any thoughts that are distracting you. Slowly put them in an imaginary cupboard for now and close the door. Return to focusing on your breath.

- See if you have an image of God. See how his face is warm and welcoming.

- Offer your full self to God right now, physically, emotionally, and spiritually. Listen. Receive whatever love and wisdom is offered for each day.

Day Two
A Tunnel in the Dan Nature Reserve

We came across this beautiful tunnel in the Dan Nature Reserve which reminds me of spiritual transformation. A tunnel is a passage or journey from one place to another, into the darkness and then out into the light. Tunnels can be carved out of rocky mountains or made with cement or stone. The length may vary, as some tunnels are short while others are much longer. So is true with spiritual growth. Some characteristics are easier to form and may take less time while others may take a long time. As I desired to be healed and transformed through a painful experience, God invited me into a journey. The darkness was difficult and yet I had faith there would be light again. Although transformation is a life-long process, I do have more confidence, courage, love, peace, and joy in my life than I ever did before.

We are created in God's image, each unique with gifts and talents. God sees each of us as his children and nothing can separate us from his love. Then we experience life. Sadly, we are hurt by people who are flawed and limited, unlike God whose love is extravagant and infinite. We internalize lies about ourselves, burying them deep inside, which creates a false sense of who we really are. God desires to uncover these lies and help you replace them with truth so you can see yourself as he sees you. When we become aware of our true selves, we can live out our purpose with confidence and experience more of the abundant life: love, joy peace, patience, kindness, faithfulness, goodness, self-control, courage, confidence, hope and internal freedom. This kind of life is open to all.

Visio Divina

- As you gaze at this picture, what speaks to you?

- Reflect on a time when you felt like you were in a dark place in life, like a dark tunnel? How did God get you into the light?

- Imagine standing at the entrance of this tunnel.
  Spend a few moments being silent or contemplative.
  Ask God to reveal any lies you believe about yourself.

- What change or growth are you hoping for?

- What do you want God to do for you?

- Journal your insights and learnings.

Day Three
Abraham's Gate (The Canaanite Gate)

I couldn't believe that Abraham was actually in this place! Abraham's gate is located in the Dan Nature Reserve. Dated back to 4,000 years ago, many believe that Abraham (previously called Abram) walked through this very gate. Our tour guide explained that this is the most impressive find of the Tel Dan excavations. Built of mud bricks, this gate had three arches that are considered to be the earliest of their kind in the world.

In Genesis 14, the story is recorded of how four kings attacked Sodom, carrying off most of the inhabitants and their possessions, including Abram's nephew, Lot. So, when Abram heard of it, he called up his 318 trained fighters and chased the four kings all the way to Dan in the far north. Abram marched right through this gate and rescued his nephew, Lot. I was inspired by Abraham's tremendous faith in God that motivated him to seek justice and that God would help him prevail.

Scripture tells us how God tested Abraham's faith. Both he and his wife, Sarah, were up in age with no children. God promised Abraham children, but Sarah just laughed at it. How could an old woman give birth? So, she talked Abraham into sleeping with their maid, who became pregnant. In other words, they didn't believe God and couldn't wait, so they took matters into their own hands. When the timing was right, Sarah did become pregnant, and they named the child Isaac. Later, Abraham was tested for his faith when God asked him to sacrifice his son. This time, Abraham did what God asked. Right as he was going to plunge the knife into Isaac, God provided a lamb instead. Such tremendous faith of Abraham and such tremendous grace from God.

How do we relate to these stories today? Sometimes, we doubt God will do what he has promised, and then we take matters in our own hands. Learning how to wait and be patient for the right timing is a challenge and yet so essential to our relationship with One whose timing is just right.

Reflection

- What stories about Abraham speak to you? (Genesis 14, 16, 21)

- What are you waiting for from God?

- Where are tempted to take matters into your own hands?

- Reflect on a time where God helped you through a difficult time. How can you trust him to be with you now in your current situation?

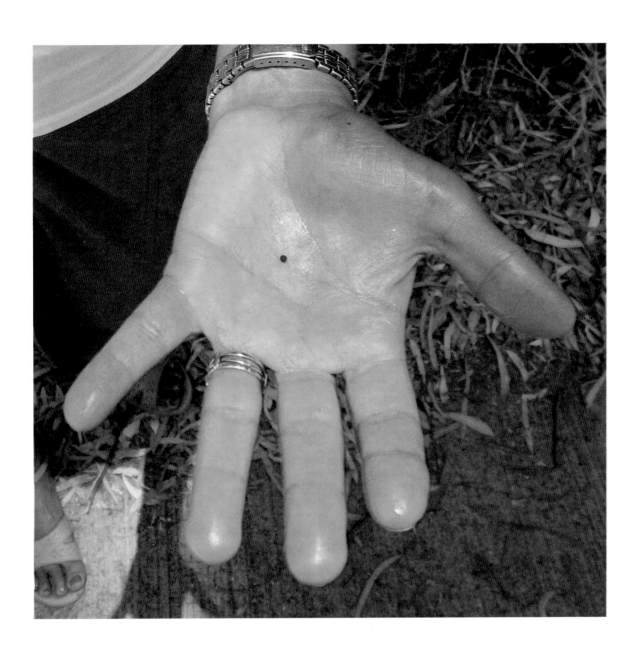

Day Four
A Mustard Seed

Can you believe how tiny this mustard seed is? Large mustard trees exist in the Dan Nature Reserve. Slowly, this tiny seed grows into a large tree where birds nestle in its branches. I was amazed that a giant tree would emerge from something so tiny. Looking back, I can see how my faith started small and has grown over the years, as my relationship with God has deepened.

Scripture Reflection

Jesus compared the mustard seed to faith and the kingdom of heaven. Read these scriptures slowly several times. Then ponder the following questions.

> *The kingdom of heaven is like to a grain of mustard seed, which a man took, and sowed in his field: which indeed is the least of all seeds: but when it is grown, it is the greatest among herbs, and becometh a tree, so that the birds of the air come and lodge in the branches thereof.*
> Matt. 13:32 KJV.

> *He replied, "Because you have so little faith. Truly I tell you, if you have faith as small as a mustard seed, you can say to this mountain, 'Move from here to there,' and it will move. Nothing will be impossible for you."* Matt. 17:20 NIV.

- What does faith like a small seed, which grows into a huge tree, mean to you?

- If your faith is strong like a huge tree, who are the birds in your life that nestle in it?

- What does Jesus mean when he says faith like a mustard seed can move a mountain?

- I believe Jesus meant that strong faith could help us get through "mountainous" obstacles in our life. What obstacles do you need faith to overcome?

- Like the mustard seed needs water and a sunny climate, what does your soul need to help you flourish?

Day Five
A Pond

We paused here for a moment by this pond in the Dan Nature Reserve. Joy filled my heart as I watched these children laughing, playing, splashing water on one another.

What children want most of all is to be loved and seen as precious by their parent(s). God desires a relationship with each one of his children (us). Sadly, some religions focus on the rules more than the relationship, leaving one to withdraw out of fear. I came up with this analogy of how God desires a relationship, not a religion.

God says to his beloved child, "I really want to spend time with you. I desire to have a great day with you at the pond: splashing each other, playing, feeling the cool water on our bodies, and laughing so hard until our stomachs hurt. Then, when we are done, we will stop and get a big ice cream cone on the way home! I love you and you are precious to me. But first, I want you to pick up your room, eat your vegetables and stop hitting your little sister. These rules are what is best for you. If you choose not to, I will feel sad, but I will love you just the same."

This is the Papa God I have come to know.

Scripture Reflection and Exercise

> *A time to weep, a time to **laugh**; a time to mourn; time to **dance**;* Ecclesiastes 3:4

- When was the last time you had fun like those children in the pond?

- What makes you laugh?

- I love to dance. When was the last time you danced? Or celebrated?

- Make a list of some activities that are fun for you. Try to do one or two this week.

- Invite God to join you in your "fun." Feel his pleasure as you two have fun together.

Day Six
Mt. Carmel

On top of Mt Carmel, my daughter pauses and takes in breathtaking views of the Jezreel valley. Nazareth is across the other side of this valley, and Megiddo is to the south. Mt. Carmel is where Elijah, the prophet, is remembered. A Carmelite monastery and church are there along with a beautiful garden in which to sit and contemplate. What touched me the most were the outstanding views from the top of this mountain. As my eyes roamed over the hills, peace and contentment roamed through my being.

Spiritual Exercise

- Spend some time at a place with a view. Pause. Take in the beauty.
  If you are not able to get out, then imagine being in the photo. Or perhaps you have a picture of a beautiful view that you can use.

- What sensations do you feel in your body?

- How does this make you feel emotionally?

- What does this view say to you about God?

- Find a place with a view to watch a sunrise. Ask God, "What is something new you have for me today? Or watch a sunset and ask, "What is something I need to let go of today?"

- Receive God's love for you, as you experience the pleasure of the view and the beautiful creation all around you.

Day Seven
Elijah

The photo shows a magnificent stone statue of Elijah, sword raised to heaven as he slaughters a Baal priest, who worshipped the false god Baal. Elijah, a highly respected prophet of God, lived in Israel and Judea in the 8th Century BC. Elijah's confrontation here on Mount Carmel with the prophets of Baal is found in I Kings 18: 30-40.

Most of us have false images about God that we are not aware of. These lies we believe about God can greatly affect our relationship with him.

> *"Our operative God image is often a subtle combination of our mom and our dad or any other significant authority figure."*
>
> Richard Rohr[3]

Most of us, often subconsciously, project our authority figures onto God. My father often raged in anger, so I subconsciously believed God was angry with me. As I have spent time with God, he has shown me he is not angry, loves me far more than I comprehend, and is truly pleased with me as his beloved daughter. Exposing any hidden lies we believe about God is crucial for building trust with him.

Reflection

- Spend some time gazing at the statue of Elijah. Write down what you notice or what speaks to you about this work of art.

- Now enter a time of silent prayer. Relax your body into your chair. Breathe in wisdom from God. Breathe out any distractions. Do this for several minutes.

- Spend the next 10 minutes or so reflecting on this question: What false beliefs or lies do I need to expose and then "slay" that keep me from drawing closer to God?

- Spend the next 10 minutes or so reflecting on this question: What are the false beliefs I need to expose and "slay" that keep me from becoming my true self?

- When you are ready, return to your body and your breathing. Slowly open your eyes. Write the insights you received in your journal.

Day Eight
Herod's pool

In the photo are the remains of Herod's swimming pool in Caesarea with a view of the Mediterranean Sea. When I swim, I feel God's pleasure. Gliding through the water brings me much joy. While swimming in the pool, I often receive insight and wisdom. When the sun peeps out from the clouds, I feel the warmth on my back. It's as if God lovingly says, "Hello, I am here." That makes me feel cherished.

A highlight for me on this trip was swimming in the Sea of Galilee, which I will share some photos later. With each stroke, I wondered, *Jesus, did you walk here? Did you fish here? Did you swim, too?* Just to swim in the lake where Jesus once walked on its surface was exhilarating to me.

"God made me fast. When I run, I feel his pleasure."
Eric Liddell, Olympic Gold Champion (1924)[4]

Spiritual Exercise

- Where do you really feel God's pleasure?

- Circle the activities that you connect with God

Church	Cooking	Writing
Community	Sewing	Books
Worship	Gardening	Work
Music	Art	Relationships
Bible	Nature	Pets
Sacraments	Travel	Eating
Service	Fishing	Creativity
Sports	Exercise	Other

- Choose an activity that gives you pleasure and invite God to join you.

23

Day Nine
Paul Appeals to Caesar

Near this circle is believed to be the actual place where the apostle Paul stood. In 58 AD, Paul was accused of starting a riot and sent to Caesarea to stand trial before the governor. According to Acts 25: 8-12, Paul stated he did nothing wrong against the Jewish or Roman law. Being a Roman citizen, Paul demanded to be tried before Caesar. After this, he sailed to Rome, where he was tried and then a few years later was executed.

To think Paul actually stood in the place was amazing. Some of his famous quotes have been daily prayers of mine.

Scripture Reflection and Prayer

*"I have **learned** by now to be quite content whatever my circumstance. I am just as happy with little as I am with much, with much as with little. I have found the recipe to be happy with whether being full or hungry, hands full or hands empty. Whatever I have, whatever I am, I can make it through anything in the One who makes me who I am."* Phil. 4: 11-13 MSG

Prayer: "Help me, God, be content with many or few."

"For by the grace given me I say to every one of you: Do not think of yourself more highly than you ought, but rather think of yourself with sober judgment, in accordance with the faith God has distributed to each of you." Romans 12:3 NIV

Prayer: "Help me, God, not to be arrogant and not to beat myself up."

"For I am convinced that neither death nor life, neither angels nor demons, neither the present nor the future, nor any powers, neither height nor depth, nor anything else in all creation, will be able to separate us from the love of God that is in Christ Jesus our Lord." Romans 8: 38-39 NIV

Prayer: "Help me, God, to know deeply in my heart, that absolutely NOTHING can separate me from your love."

- Spend some time reflecting on these scriptures. What is God saying to you?
- Take the above prayers and say them with a single breath.

Day Ten
Gabriel Appearing to Mary

Have you ever seen an angel? I have not; however, gazing at these statues of Gabriel appearing to Mary in front of the Basilica of Annunciation in Nazareth, reminded me of a richly transformational experience I had with the Spiritual Exercises of St. Ignatius. Through an Imaginative Prayer of Gabriel appearing to Mary, God asked me to let go of my fear and share my story of childhood trauma and healing. I related to Mary's fear of being shunned from her community since she was pregnant out of wedlock, which was not acceptable in those days. Yet, she didn't allow what other people thought or would do to hold her back. Filled with this lovingly rich experience from God, she stepped out in courage and said, "Yes" to him to be the mother of Jesus. And I stepped out and said, "Yes" to share my story of how God has slowly stitched my childhood wounds. A scar remains, but the pain is gone. Words cannot express the gratitude I feel towards God and for saying "Yes" to him.

Imaginative Prayer

- Read the passage in Luke: 1:26-28, slowly several times.

- Find a quiet place. Close your eyes. Relax your body. Breathe deeply.

- Imagine you are in this scene. You may be the angel or an observer.

- What is God saying to you?

- Try to be Mary. Or if you are a man, try to be Joseph. His story is on Day 11. Although he is not in this passage, he was asked to be the earthly father of Jesus and said "Yes" to God.

- What is something new that God wants to "birth" inside of you?

- How do you relate to Mary's response, "How can this really happen?"

- What fear or obstacle is holding you back from saying "Yes" to God? Talk to him about it.

- Like Mary and Joseph, how can you be empowered, take courage, step out, and fulfill your purpose?

- Take some time to journal your insights from God.

Day 11
The Chapel of Joseph

Here is the small Chapel of St. Joseph, built near the Basilica of Annunciation. I sat in the back of this Chapel of St. Joseph and reflected on the following passage in Matthew 1:18-24.

> [18] This is how the birth of Jesus the Messiah came about: his mother Mary was pledged to be married to Joseph, but before they came together, she was found to be pregnant through the Holy Spirit. [19] Because Joseph her husband was faithful to the law, and yet did not want to expose her to public disgrace, he had in mind to divorce her quietly.
> [20] But after he had considered this, an angel of the Lord appeared to him in a dream and said, "Joseph son of David, do not be afraid to take Mary home as your wife, because what is conceived in her is from the Holy Spirit. [21] She will give birth to a son, and you are to give him the name Jesus, because he will save his people from their sins."
> [22] All this took place to fulfill what the Lord had said through the prophet: [23] "The virgin will conceive and give birth to a son, and they will call him Immanuel" (which means "God with us").
> [24] When Joseph woke up, he did what the angel of the Lord had commanded him and took Mary home as his wife.

What spoke to me was the integrity of Joseph. First, he had to listen to his betrothed tell him she was pregnant, and this was a miraculous conception by God. Back in those days, sex outside of marriage was not accepted in their culture. I wonder what he was thinking. Anger at her betrayal? Disgusted by her getting pregnant? Shocked that she made up this God-is-the-father-by-a-miracle story?

Instead of telling her off or disgracing her publicly, he decided to break it off with her quietly. *Such grace!* Until God told him what she said was true, and he was to marry her. Joseph did not argue with God or talk about Mary behind her back. He did the right thing and said, "Yes" to God.

Scripture Reflection

- Read the above passage slowly several times.

- What does being a man or woman of integrity look like to you?

- What is God asking of you, even though it may be difficult to comprehend?

- Perhaps something else is speaking to you through this story. Journal what you learned.

Day 12
Ruins of Nazareth

I stood here in awe, looking at these ancient ruins of Nazareth, wondering what it must have been like for Jesus as a child, running through the cobblestone streets, playing, laughing with other children. What about his young adult years, sitting on those stone benches, talking, listening, "hanging out" with friends? I found myself wanting to know more about those years in his life.

I spent time reflecting on my own story. God was with me in both the most joyful and most painful experiences of my life. Recalling where I felt his love for me brought joy to my heart. Our story is a powerful tool for seeing how God is present throughout our lives.

Spiritual Practice: Write Your Story

- Describe your home growing up. What was it like?
- Describe your parents, grandparents, siblings and other relatives. What were they like? What messages did you receive from them about life? About God?
- Write the highlights of your school years. Who was your favorite teacher, and why? Your least favorite teacher, and why? What did you learn about yourself or God through both of them?
- What did you learn about God through church, clergy or mentors?
- Write about major milestones: graduation, career, marriage, children, grandchildren, retirement, etc. How have these influenced your spiritual life?
- Write about the 3-4 best events/experiences in your life. Reflect on what you wrote, then answer the following questions:
  > How was God there? Where did you feel His love for you?
  > What did you learn? How have you grown?
  > Was there a turning point in your faith?
- Express gratitude for all the gifts and answered prayers (both big and small) God gave you during the best events.
- Write about the 3-4 worst/most painful events in your life. *If this triggers PTSD, then please refrain. Or choose those events that you feel comfortable writing about.* Reflect on what you wrote, then reflect on these questions:
  > How was God there for you? Where did you feel His presence?
  > Was there a turning point in your faith?
  > How have you grown?
  > Is God safe for you?
- In your own words, express gratitude for how you survived, how you were able to get through and to God for being there with you, even though it didn't feel like it.

Day 13
The Jordan River

This is a photo of The Banias Falls, near the source of three rivers that form the Jordan River. Having spiritual significance for both Jewish and Christian pilgrims because the Israelites crossed The Jordan River to enter the promised land, and Jesus was baptized in the river.

I love getting out in nature, soaking in the beauty, breathing in the fresh air, smelling the water or flowers, and feeling the sun and the wind on my face. Being in God's creation connects me more deeply to him. I am amazed at his artwork and his creativity. Such a tremendous gift to us.

Although this is not the location, I imagined Jesus being baptized here. One of my favorite passages is The Baptism of Jesus. When I do an Imaginative Prayer with this passage, I hear God saying to me that I am his beloved daughter, with whom he is well pleased.

> *At that time, Jesus came from Nazareth in Galilee and was baptized by John in the Jordan. As Jesus was coming up out of the water, he saw heaven being torn open and the Spirit descending on him like a dove. And a voice came from heaven: "You are my Son, whom I love; with you I am well pleased."*   Mark 1:9-13 (NIV)

Spiritual Exercise: Practicing God's Presence in Nature

- Find a beautiful place in nature to sit or even take a walk. This could be in your own backyard. Ponder the following questions:

- As you sit quietly in nature, what do you notice? Use your five senses.

- What are the characteristics you enjoy about the _____? (ocean, park, desert, river, garden, etc.).

- How do these characteristics relate to God?

- How does God reveal himself to you through the _____?

- How does being here at the _____ make you feel?

- What is God inviting you into?

Breath Prayer

- In a single breath, pray *I am God's son/daughter, with whom he is well pleased.*

Day 14
Cana

Here you see some ancient water jugs like the ones they used in Jesus' time. Changing water into wine, *really good wine,* was Jesus' first miracle in Cana, as told in John 2:1-12. What I noticed is that even Jesus took time out to celebrate. I can't think of a more fun, joyous party, big celebration than a wedding. Everyone is happy. Especially the bride and groom.

Looking at these ancient jars reminds me of spiritual transformation. Although grapes are delicious, there is something so much more for them. When juicy and plump, the grapes are harvested. Then the grapes must be crushed. With each stomp, a flavorful juice emerges. Over time, the juice becomes fermented inside a keg. Then the day comes to pour the wine into a bottle, cork it, and store it in a cellar until the time it is ready to be enjoyed.

Our journey can be similar. There is so much more for you if you are willing to allow God to enter those places in your heart that need healing, growth, and change. It might feel like being *crushed* at times, but God is with you, molding you into the person he created you to be. You will notice a change, more internal freedom, which will lead to joy and celebration like that of a wedding!

Spiritual Exercise

- Pour yourself a glass of wine, non-alcoholic wine, or glass of grape juice.
  Smell the aromas as you swish the wine/juice in the glass. Invite God to join you for what I call "Happy Hour."

  Take a sip and savor that in your mouth. Feel it slowly move its way into your stomach as you swallow. While you enjoy this glass of wine or juice, ponder the process of changing grapes into wine or grape juice. Dwell on the transformation process from pruning the vine, watering the grapes, harvesting, crushing, fermenting, to finally being able to taste and enjoy.

  As you compare this process to your spiritual life, where are you at?
  Talk to God about it as you would a friend.

Day 15
The Church of Cana

This photo is of my husband and I renewing our vows in the church at Cana on our actual anniversary date! At that time, we'd been married 28 years. With a strong desire to renew my vows on this day, I felt so disappointed with all the busloads of people inside the church. I prayed and asked God to make a way for us to have some quiet. And then within minutes, the whole church became empty! Hurrying to the front of the church, we renewed our vows to one another with our grown daughters beside us. A whole ten minutes of quiet. Just as we finished our last vow, a busload of people entered. This was one of those times I mentioned previously about God often clearing the crowds for me. *Gratitude filled my heart for both the ten minutes and twenty-eight years.*

Spiritual Practice: Renewing Your Vow with God

- Where is your relationship with God right now?

- Are you at the dating stage? Just getting to know each other, excited and yet unsure?

- Or the honeymoon stage, where there is euphoria all around, and you desire to be together 24/7?

- Perhaps at a busy stage; raising kids, work, buying a home with very little time to spend together.

- Are you like that couple who is married but not speaking? Sleeping in separate bedrooms? Just married on paper?

- Have you settled into a boring routine? Perhaps you need a different or new way to connect with God, to pray, or to be with him?

- Or maybe you are like that content, loving couple, who share both ups and downs together.

- Desire from both spouses is necessary for the marriage to grow deeper. God has a deep desire to draw closer to you.

  What about you?

30. 10. 2

Day 16
Jacob's Well

This photo is of the original Jacob's well, dating back thousands of years ago. It is located in the city of Nablus, near the archaeological site of Tel Balata, which was the biblical site of Shechem. Sadly, I was not able to visit this place since it was not safe then. Our friend, Domingo Cabrera, visited this site in 2016 and gave me permission to use his photos. He said there was not much to see in this tiny village except for the Greek Orthodox church that was built over the well. Being deeply moved, Domingo felt that Jesus actually sat here.

I love the story of Jesus and the Samaritan woman, as told in John 4. Jesus was headed back to Galilee and traveled through Samaria. As he sat by Jacob's well, a woman came up to draw water. In those days, Jews despised Samaritans and did not speak to them. Scripture says she was a sinful woman and most likely treated as an outcast. But Jesus didn't care what other people thought. He did not judge her for being a different race. He spoke to her anyway. Although he called her out on her behavior, he didn't *shame* her for sleeping with different men. Instead, he offered her *Living Water.* In other words, a relationship with him, freedom from shame, and eternal life. Being so overjoyed with this experience, she ran to tell the others in her village. She even left her precious water jug there, which is like me leaving my purse!

The grace and love that Jesus showed the Samaritan woman that day reminds me of the same love he has shown me. Before we can get close to someone, we need to know they love us, accept us for who we are, not criticize us for our shortcomings and truly want God's best for us. *This is the Jesus I know.*

Imaginative Prayer

- Read through John 4 slowly. Allow at least 15 min. to do these next steps. You may want to look over the questions below before you close your eyes.

- Now close your eyes and use your imagination. Put yourself in this scene. Or you can look at the photos above. Use your senses. What do you see? Hear? Smell?

- Try being the Samaritan woman (or man). As you walk towards the well, you see Jesus sitting there. With warm and welcoming eyes, he invites you to sit at the well and listen. What is he saying to you?

- He does not shame you for having 5 spouses, or whatever it is you have done. How does this make you feel?

- See him looking at you with this gaze of love. How do you feel that Jesus wants to be with you, a Samaritan? Sit for a while and receive his gift of love and living water.

Day 17
The Mount of Beatitudes

Some believe Jesus gave his famous sermon on the mount here, while others believe the actual location is unknown. The Roman Catholics built this church in 1937-38 on the northwestern shore of the Sea of Galilee, now called The Mount of the Beatitudes. Today, the spacious grounds are filled with beautifully groomed trees, fragrant flowers, and a variety of places to sit and contemplate, as you will see in the next photos. I spent my time sitting quietly and reflecting on the Beatitudes as written in Matthew 5:3-11.

I invite you to do the same. I will list the beatitudes with the New International version on top and The Message version below, and then a reflection question for you to ponder. Or God may invite you to ponder something else that springs forth from this famous sermon.

Scripture Reflection

3 *"Blessed are the poor in spirit, for theirs is the kingdom of heaven."*

   "You are blessed when you are at the end of your rope. With less of you, there is more of God and his rule."

- Someone once said true humility is not thinking less of yourself. It is thinking of yourself…less. How can you become humble, so God can be more?

4 *"Blessed are those who mourn, for they will be comforted."*

   "You're blessed when you feel you've lost what is most dear to you. Only then can you be embraced by the One most dear to you."

- What are you mourning over? What or who have you lost in life that was most dear to you? Ask God to embrace you.

5 *"Blessed are the meek, for they will inherit the earth."*

   "You're blessed when you're content with just who you are—no more, no less. That's the moment you find yourselves proud owners of everything that can't be bought."

- What are you content with about who you are? If you are discontent, what is that about? If you do struggle with this, try to embrace the truth that you are created in God's image, beautifully made, gifted with talents to fulfill your purpose.

6 *"Blessed are those who hunger and thirst for righteousness, for they will be filled."*

"You're blessed when you've worked up a good appetite for God. He's food and drink in the best meal you'll ever eat."

- What are you hungry for from God?

- What does thirst for righteousness look like to you?

7 *" Blessed are the merciful, for they will be shown mercy."*

"You're blessed when you care. At the moment of being 'care-full,' you find yourselves cared for."

- Reflect on a time when someone showed you mercy.

- Reflect on a time when you showed someone mercy.

- Whether you received or offered mercy, how did that make you feel?

8 *"Blessed are the pure in heart, for they will see God."*

"You're blessed when you get your inside world—your mind and heart—put right. Then you can see God in the outside world."

- What impure thoughts are you having?

- Dwell and meditate on what is right, true, and noble. Whatever you dwell on will slowly sink into your heart.

9 *"Blessed are the peacemakers, for they will be called children of God."*

"You're blessed when you can show people how to cooperate instead of compete or fight. That's when you discover who you really are, and your place in God's family."

- What peace do you need in your life now?

- How can you be an example or teach cooperation instead of arguing?

10 *"Blessed are those who are persecuted because of righteousness, for theirs is the kingdom of heaven."*

"You're blessed when your commitment to God provokes persecution. The persecution drives you even deeper into God's kingdom."

11-12 *"Blessed are you when people insult you, persecute you and falsely say all kinds of evil against you because of me. Rejoice and be glad, because great is your reward in heaven, for in the same way, they persecuted the prophets who were before you."*

"Not only that — count yourselves blessed every time people put you down or throw you out or speak lies about you to discredit me. What it means is that the truth is too close for comfort and they are uncomfortable. You can be glad when that happens — give a cheer, even! — for though they don't like it, I do! And all heaven applauds. And know that you are in good company. My prophets and witnesses have always gotten into this kind of trouble."

- When have you been slandered, ostracized, gossiped about, treated poorly, left out, or suffered bodily harm because of your faith?

- How did this make you feel?

- How did God help you get through that?

- How did you grow closer to God through that?

Day 18
Church of Multiplication

The Church of Multiplication is in Tabgha, along the Northwest shore of the Sea of Galilee. Here, inside the church, is the altar that was built over a rock, where many believe Jesus fed the 5,000. This modern Catholic church was built on the site of a 4th-century church. Beautiful floor mosaics were discovered during the excavations, including the one by the altar of two fish and five loaves of bread.

In this story (John 6:1-12), Jesus miraculously fed thousands of hungry and poor people from just two fish and five loaves of bread. What spoke to me was that Jesus knew he was going to perform a miracle, and yet he still asked his disciples how they were going to feed all these people. They didn't know what to do and said they did not have enough money. Even though the disciples witnessed other miracles, their faith was still limited. Jesus asked this young boy to share all he had. Willingly, this lad offered his only food to God, who took it, blessed it, and multiplied it beyond anything imaginable. And with enough food left over!

Like the disciples, I can wonder what to do. When I published my first book, I was surprised that it reached people in Africa and Australia. God reminded me to trust that he will multiply my books to reach those who are hungry for healing.

Scripture Reflection

- Spend time reading and reflecting on the story told in Matt. 14:13-21 or John 6:1-14 of feeding the 5,000 people.

- What is God saying to you through this story?

- What would you like to have multiplied in your life?

- How can you trust God, that he will multiply his purpose through your small offering?

Day 19
Capernaum

Filled with anticipation and excitement, I entered the City of Jesus. The ruins of Capernaum were first discovered in 1836. It was a fishing village along the northern shore of the Sea of Galilee. Jesus spent much time in the town of Capernaum. He taught in the synagogue, healed the sick, cast out demons, and spent time enjoying people. This is also the town where Peter was from and with whom Jesus stayed when he was not traveling to other towns.

Many of his healing miracles were performed in this small town long ago. Some of these include:

- Healing the Official's Son (John 4:43-54)
- Healing Peter's Mother-in-law of a Fever (Mark 1:29-31)
- Healing a Centurion's Paralyzed Servant (Luke 7:1-10)
- Healing the Man with the Shriveled Hand (Matthew 12:9-14)
- Healing a Demon Possessed Man (Luke 4:31-36)

One of my favorites is the Healing of the Leper as told in Mark 1:40-42. NLT.

> *A man with leprosy came and knelt down in front of Jesus, begging to be healed.*
> *"If you are willing, you can heal me and make me clean."*
> *Moved with compassion, Jesus reached out and touched him. "I am willing," he said. "Be healed!"*
> *Instantly, the leprosy disappeared, and the man was healed.*

I love how compassionate Jesus was when he saw this leper. Not only were lepers banned from society because they were contagious, but they were also labeled "unclean." Back then, people believed that sin caused a disease, illness or handicap. Jesus didn't discriminate when he healed people. The Jews hated being under Roman rule, and yet Jesus healed the Centurion's servant. Time and time again, I notice that Jesus was not "selective," not caring what other people thought. He still sees each person as a child of God and feels compassion when they are suffering.

Some people struggle with this passage who have not been healed, thinking Jesus is not willing. I don't have answers for why one person is healed, and another person is not, but it is certainly not because Jesus doesn't care about you or is not willing. Our friend, Ted, has ALS. After months of struggling with God, begging for healing, Ted has accepted this horrible disease that has taken over his body. He told us that his relationship with God is deeper than it ever has been, and he is able to experience joy. Not the joy that is associated with happiness, but an attitude that God is with him always, helping him through this, and loves him deeply.

If Ted can experience God's grace in the midst of deep suffering, then so can I, and so can you.

Imaginative Prayer

- Choose one of the above passages and do an Imaginative Prayer. May you feel God's love and compassion for you. Journal your experience.

THE LATE FOURTH CENTURY A.D
"WHITE SYNAGOGUE"
BUILT UPON THE REMAINS OF THE
"SYNAGOGUE OF JESUS"

Day 20
The Synagogue of Jesus

I felt so excited to be in the place where Jesus worshiped, taught, and met in community with others. Excavations led to the discovery of two ancient Synagogues. One was the 4th Century "White Synagogue" built over the original foundation of the Synagogue of Jesus.

You can see the bottom layer of the floor that was a part of the original synagogue during Jesus' time with two original steps. Pausing on those two steps, thinking Jesus had done the same, I felt goosebumps all over my arms!

I reflected on the Sabbath. Genesis tells us that God created the world and then rested on the 7th day. The fourth commandment is to keep the Sabbath day holy. In Mark 2:27, Jesus said *the Sabbath was made for man, not man for the Sabbath.*

Sabbath means *Stop* or *Cease.* Take a break. Rest. Relax. God created the world, and then he rested. *And he was God!* Jesus took time out to rest, nap, and be alone with God. We were created with the need for sleep, to relax, and to rest. Such a health benefit, too!

Today, there are differences among religious traditions on how the Sabbath is observed. When I was in Israel, the orthodox Jews still practice no work of any kind on the Sabbath. Our hotel had a Shabbat elevator that would stop on each floor and automatically open the door since pushing a button caused an electric spark, which is considered work. I felt this was somewhat extreme. However, in my culture, there is the opposite extreme, and many do not rest on the Sabbath at all. Work-aholism has become an idol in the United States.

The world was forced to cease during COVID19. Worry and fear dominated the hearts of many who became sick with the virus as well as those who lost their jobs. Some felt so isolated, craving a hug from a loved one. Then there were those who were content, feeling less fatigued by not having to drive in traffic. Having more time to reflect and think, they could see what was dragging them down and how much more joy they felt without all the hustle and bustle. One told me her mind was less cluttered, having more time to reflect and be with God. Taking a rest or slowing down became a welcomed "New Normal." As a spiritual director, I asked my directees and myself, "What 'New Normal' will you take with you when the 'Old Normal' starts up again?" Hopefully, it will include a Shabbat.

Spiritual Exercise: Shabbat

- How do you practice the Sabbath?

- What are your beliefs about rest? Circle those that apply:

  Beneficial   Lazy   Unproductive   Healthy   Waste of time
  Nourishing   Necessary   Enjoyable   Unnecessary

- Look at your life. What can you say "No" to so you can have more time to rest?

- Take time out to rest, relax, and replenish your soul.

Day 21
The White Synagogue

Here you see in the ruins of the White Synagogue, a group of Catholic seminary students from Ireland. They were so friendly to me. I watched them as they sang together, shared communion, and prayed The Our Father. They also took time to be alone with God, then returned to share their experiences with one another. What a beautiful example of community.

Prayer: The Our Father

The Our Father (Matthew 6:9-13) is written here, along with a version I wrote below.

The Our Father

Our Father in heaven
Hallowed be thy name
Your kingdom come
Your will be done
On earth as it is in heaven
Give us today our daily bread
Forgive us our debts as we also forgive our debtors
And lead us not into temptation
But deliver us from the evil one

Our Father who art in heaven, hallowed be thy name.
Father, I praise you for _____.

Your kingdom come, your will be done on earth as it is in heaven.
What is your will for me today, God? _____.

Give us this day our daily bread.
I pray for _____ and for myself for what I/we need today _____.

Forgive us our debts as we also forgive our debtors.
 Forgive me for_____. Forgive _____ for _____.

And lead us not into temptation.
Help me not be tempted by _____.

But deliver us from the evil one. Amen.

Day 22
Healing of the Paraplegic

One of my favorite stories that happened here in the village was the Healing of the Paraplegic, as told in Luke 5:18-25. In the photo are the remains of the village of Capernaum, next to the White Synagogue. These four friends carried a paraplegic man on his mat to where Jesus was preaching in a home. Since it was too crowded to enter through the door, the friends went up on the roof, possibly by some stairs, and lowered their friend down to where Jesus was. Amazed at their faith, Jesus healed the man, freed him from sin, and then told him to take his mat and walk.

I was moved by the four friends. Since it meant healing for their friend, they were willing to do an extremely difficult task. I am blessed to be a part of a small group of soul friends where we have been "carrying our mats" for each other over the last eight years. *Such a treasured gift!*

Imaginative Prayer

- Read the story slowly, several times, with one time being out loud, as told in Luke 5:18-25.

- Imagine Jesus is teaching in this home you see in the picture. The house is jammed packed full of people. Where in your life do you feel you cannot "get in" to get your needs met?

- Who are your soul friends that help carry your mat? Who encourages you to draw closer to Jesus? Say something to each person of what you appreciate about them.

- Now imagine laying on your mat, and your friends come up with a plan to lower you down into the house through the roof. There are stairs that lead up to the roof. What are you thinking about this? Do you admire their boldness or are you afraid they will drop you?

- Your friends carry you up safely on the roof. Now they are lowering you down until you are at eye level with Jesus. What is the expression on his face as he looks at you?

- What do you need forgiven? He compassionately says you are forgiven.

- Now he offers healing. What healing do you need?

- Now he tells you to pick up your mat, walk and go. What do you feel as you walk out of there?

- Before you go, spend time expressing gratitude to Jesus for the freedom through forgiveness and healing. And to your four spiritual companions who came alongside you. Journal your experience.

Day 23
Peter's House

This photo shows the ruins, which many believe was the house of Peter. During excavations, some stones inscribed with Peter's name were discovered, and the Catholics built a church over this house to preserve the remains. He was one of Jesus' closest disciples and a fisherman by trade. Jesus healed his mother-in-law of illness, so we know he was married, although we don't know anything about his wife.

What do you think of when you think of Peter? Peter came across as bold, fearless, outspoken and yet soon crumbled when faced with fear. When he started to walk on the Sea of Galilee, fear rose up, and he almost drowned. After witnessing the glorious transfiguration, he suggested putting up shelters on Mt. Hermon, so they could stay there forever; however, Jesus knew he had to go to the cross. I actually agree with Peter. Who wants to suffer? Transformation can be painful at times, but healing and emotional wellness result by going through pain. Then Peter tried to be so bold as to cut off the soldier's ear who arrested Jesus. Not realizing that in just a short time, fear would rise up again, leading him to deny his best friend three times.

There was hope for Peter. After the resurrection, being filled with the Holy Spirit, courage, boldness, and faith were genuinely deepened in him. When fear welled up, it was suddenly squelched as evidenced by the acts of courage and faith that Peter displayed when he was beaten, imprisoned, persecuted and finally executed for his faith. *Fear no longer held him back.*

Spiritual Exercise: Power Walk of Courage

- Take a power walk. Leave the iPod behind. Walk in silence, follow the suggestions, and ponder these questions.

- Hold your head up high as you walk. Where do you need courage in your life? Name it.

- Pound the pavement as you walk, feeling stronger with each step. Where do you need to be empowered and take your life back?

- Feel your breath quicken as you walk. What is something bold you want to say or do? Say it in your breath over and over.

- Bend your arms up to your side, clench your fists. Swing your arms back and forth. What is holding you back? Name your fear. Punch that fear with each swing of your arm.

- Find some stairs. Or a small hill. Go up and down, as best you can. What steps can you take to be filled with courage, faith, and boldness? Ask God to fill you with his spirit.

- When you finish your walk, journal your insights.

Day 24
Calling of Levi

Sitting on this bench, gazing out over the Sea of Galilee, gave me such tremendous peace. I wondered where Jesus taught from the boat or walked on the water. Settling in, I chose to contemplate on the *Calling of Levi and Eating with Sinners* as told in Mark 2:13-17. Tax collectors were despised during the time of Jesus and socializing with them was heavily frowned upon. But Jesus didn't care what others thought. He spent time with those who wanted what he had to offer, and he did not judge or criticize them for their failings. Jesus even asked this one tax collector, Levi, to become a disciple. Later, he was called Matthew, who eventually wrote one of the gospels. I love how Jesus looked beyond the sin in Levi's life and saw the amazing man (and author) that God created him to be.

Jesus tells us not to judge one another. We need to take a good look in the mirror and clean our own face before we try to wipe the face of another. There is a difference between being "judgy" and being "discerning." If I am with a controlling person, it is healthy to discern this and put up appropriate boundaries. If I criticize or attack their character, then this is being "judgy." There was a time that someone told me I was judgmental when I disagreed with them. I wasn't condemning them for their point of view but trying to express my own. Now I suggest to "agree to disagree," which allows people to have different opinions (which we all do) while not attacking each other's character.

Jesus said the second greatest commandment is to treat others as you want to be treated. Since I don't like being judged, then I try not to do the same. Also, I try not to be "judgy" towards myself.

Spiritual Exercise

- Name someone in your life you feel judged or criticized by. How does this make you feel?

- Is this difference in opinions or beliefs?

- What is going on in their life? Try to put yourself in their shoes. This doesn't make it right; it just helps to understand.

- Maybe the person isn't being critical; they just need to be right. The more mature we are, we can have our opinions and beliefs and let go of the need for the other person to agree with us.

- How can you show kindness with appropriate boundaries?

- Now name someone (or group of people) you tend to judge. Ask yourself: When I judge, what is my tone? Is it condemning or am I discerning?

- If I am judgmental, ask why? What is this about? Am I taking it personally? Do I need to be right? Do I have unrealistic expectations of this person?

- How do you judge or criticize yourself? Why? Offer yourself compassion. We are all "works in progress."

DAY 25
A Boat Ride on the Sea of Galilee

With a beautiful view from my hotel balcony of the Sea of Galilee, I could see several boats full of pilgrims, just like this one. I reflected on the story of Jesus calming the storm (Mark 4:35-41). A giant storm arose, tossing the disciple's boat from side to side. As fear filled their hearts, they cried out to Jesus for help. Immediately, he calmed the storm. They were amazed that Jesus even had power over the sea.

I don't live in a place where we huge storms, but I have felt fear caused by the storms of life, some of which were not even true. Several years ago, a letter came in the mail one day after a routine mammogram. Inside in bold letters: THE RESULTS WERE ABNORMAL. Fear rose up, and I started to worry. Before the end of the day, I had my funeral all planned out. I went back to have a sonogram. The Doctor said it was just a cyst. See you next year.

What a wasted time of energy! So, I decided to fast worry and making false assumptions for lent. After experiencing much more peace, I chose to make this a new habit. What I do now is "Hold a Valid Concern" while not playing the "What if?" videotape. So, is it normal to be concerned about our storms in life? Absolutely. But creating a false, made-up-scenario in our head creates an inner storm like no other.

Spiritual Practice: Calming the Inner Storm

- Identify what your fears are right now.

- What is causing this inner storm in you?

- If you are playing the "What if?" video, ask yourself: Is this true? Do I have the facts? Will this really happen?

- If there is some truth, then "Hold a Valid Concern" until you know it is true.

- If there is no truth or uncertainty, then *let it go.*

- Practice being present. Look at the picture of the boat on the Sea of Galilee. Imagine being on that boat. It is calm now. What else do you see? What do you smell? Hear? Touch?

- Try deep breathing. Therapists suggest four breaths a minute. Breathing deeply sends a message to the heart to slow down, which sends a message to the brain to calm down.

- Sink into your chair. Imagine you are sinking into "Trusting God." As the chair holds and comforts you, trust that God is doing the same during this storm in your life.

- As Jesus had power over the storm, ask for power to calm your inner storm.

DAY 26
Migdal

The ancient village of Migdal was recently discovered in 1986. This was not open at the time I was there, but it was when Irene visited. She stated that someone had bought the land to build a shopping center. When they started to dig, these ruins were discovered and became a historical site. Migdal or Magdala was the town where Mary Magdalene was from. Luke 8:2 tells us that Jesus cast seven demons out of her. Experiencing this internal freedom, she became a devout follower of Christ. She is often confused with being a prostitute. But I agree with scholars that believe she was not and possibly supported Jesus' ministry with both finances and service to others. I admire how she was there for Jesus at the cross when the others had all fled in fear, except for John. Here is her story that I have adapted from the scriptures.

"You can't imagine what I have been through. I was in torment day and night by seven demons ravaging my soul. Unbearable anger, addiction, fear, hatred, bitterness, and resentment filled my being like being in chains with no hope of a key.

Until the day Jesus came into my village. With great boldness and compassion, he called those demons out, one by one. My body collapsed to the ground, completely exhausted and yet totally free. I followed him from that day on.

He did so many wonderful miracles! Demons were cast out of people, just like me. The lame could walk, and the blind could see. He even raised Lazarus from the dead! Thousands were fed with just two fish and five loaves of bread. And the teachings from his mouth were like warm, homemade bread to my soul.

Then that horrible, dreadful day came. Falsely accused, arrested, beaten, flogged, mocked, he was led away like a lamb awaiting to be slaughtered. I stood there at the cross, wailing in tears with the other women, slowly watching each breath leave his body.

We didn't even have time to give him a proper burial. So early that Sunday morning, I went to the tomb with my spices, only to find his body was missing! Seeing this gardener, I pleaded through my tears as to where he moved the body. Then suddenly, he gently and lovingly called my name, *"Mary."*

My Rabboni (Teacher) stood there, alive, before my eyes! Tears of despair quickly melted into tears of joy. *I have seen the Lord!"*

Spiritual Exercise

- What speaks to you about Mary Magdalene?
- Is there something you desire freedom from bondage over?
- Who was there for you during your darkest time? How did that make you feel?
- Name an event where despair turned into extreme happiness.
- What stirs inside of you as Jesus reveals himself to you and says your name?

Day 27
Caesarea Philippi

Caesarea Philippi was an ancient Roman city in northern Israel, located at the southwestern base of Mount Hermon. Several shrines were built dedicated to the Greek god Pan and to Caesar. The top photo shows what this city looked like long ago, and the bottom photo is what remains today.

In Matthew 16:13-20, Jesus asks his disciples who the people here think he is. They replied, John the Baptist, Elijah, or some other prophet. Then Jesus asks Peter who he thinks he is. Peter replies, Christ, the son of God.

Who do you say he is?

Scripture Reflection

² I am the Lord your God, who brought you out of Egypt, out of the land of slavery.
³ You shall have no other gods before me.
⁴ You shall not make for yourself an image in the form of anything in heaven above or on the earth beneath or in the waters below.   Exodus 20:2-4a

Jesus replied: "Love the Lord your God with all your heart and with all your soul and with all your mind."   Matthew 22:37

- Ask God, "What do I love more than you?" "Who or what do I worship?"
  Perhaps it is not a god like Pan, but could be money, power, prestige, praise, admiration from people, or ego.

- What competes in your heart from loving God? Doubt? Hatred? Greed? Jealousy? Other?

- What competes in your mind from loving God? Negativity? Prejudice? False assumptions? False image of God? Selfishness? Other?

- What competes in your body? Addictions? Neglect? Rage?

- If you are not sure, ask someone close to you what is really most important to you. Sometimes, others can see what we cannot. Or look at what you fantasize about or think about all the time. This can give you insight into your idols.

Day 28
Beit She'an

The ancient Philistine city of Beit She'an was on this site. The ruins you see are from a Roman city built later. At the time of Christ, this was called Scythopolis and was one of the ten Decapolis Cities mentioned in the Bible. The Philistine city now lies under that hill you see in the photo, known as a Tel. Our guide told us that underneath the Tel is the Philistine wall where the bodies of Saul and his sons were hung after a battle, as told in 1 Chronicles 10. There were ten Decapolis Cities at the time of Jesus. He traveled through some of them, preaching and healing. Although I am not sure which city this happened in, one of my favorite stories is Jesus healing the deaf man.

> *After he took him aside, away from the crowd, Jesus put his fingers into the man's ears. Then he spit and touched the man's tongue. He looked up to heaven and with a deep sigh said to "Ephphatha!" (which means "Be opened!"). At this, the man's ears were opened, his tongue was loosened, and he began to speak plainly.* Mark 7:31-37.

Prior to becoming a Spiritual Director, I was an Audiologist. Helping people hear was a passion of mine. Watching a deaf child's eyes light up when they first hear a sound through amplification brought me such joy. After I retired, my passion was to become a certified spiritual director. This is more about accompanying someone rather than directing. I am honored to hear what God is doing in people's lives. By offering my presence, compassionate listening, open-ended questions and encouragement, the directee can explore their experiences and deepen their relationship with God. I moved from helping people hear their outer world to listening to their inner world.

Scripture Reflection
- Read the scripture above out loud in Mark 7:33-35a. Listen to the words as you speak.
- What in your mind needs to be opened? What in your heart needs to be opened? Listen.

Practice: Compassionate Listening
- There is a time to talk and a time to listen. Most people do not listen well. Notice if you are talking too much. Ask God what that is about.

- Genuinely ask people how they are doing. Ask open ended questions. Nod your head or reflect a few words they say back to them, so they know you are listening.

- Maintain eye contact. Don't look at your phone. Do not interrupt and make it about you. Concentrate what on the person is saying, not what you are going to say next.

- *Be open* to what the person is sharing. Try not to judge what they say. Remember we all have different opinions and beliefs. See them as God's beloved just as you are

Day 29
Qumran Caves

Archaeologists discovered a series of caves in 1946, which lie near Wadi Qumran. The remains of multiple Hebrew scrolls were discovered, dating from more than 100 years before Christ. These became known as the Dead Sea Scrolls. One of those scrolls is an early copy of the Book of Isaiah, which resides in the Israel Museum in Jerusalem and is not allowed to be photographed. The scroll you see in the next photo is a replica. What amazed me was this copy closely resembles the Masoretic Text, the authoritative text of the Hebrew Bible, which was written 1,000 years later. This tells me that the Bible we have today is the same as it has been for thousands of years.

The Book of Isaiah is the first of the Major Prophets in the Old Testament. The book begins by establishing the themes of judgment and consequent renewal for the righteous. Isaiah was held in such a high regard that the book was sometimes referred to as "the Fifth Gospel," the prophet who wrote more precisely of Christ and the Church than any others.

We were the only visitors there. My tour guide kept saying there are usually 13 buses here and couldn't believe we had the whole place to ourselves. I just smiled and expressed my gratitude to the same God that Isaiah wrote about long ago. *Thank you, God. I love you, too.*

Personal Reflection

- As you can see in the photo, the Qumran Caves are out in the middle of the desert. These caves are empty now, but once filled with buried treasure; a copy of the Book of Isaiah. This book has blessed and encouraged so many people over the years and still today. What are some of your favorite verses/passages in Isaiah?

- God has placed treasured gifts and talents in each one of us. Are yours hidden inside your cave? What is keeping them buried?

- We all have something to offer. Ask God to help you release your treasure inside. There are so many people who will be blessed by what you have to offer.

- The Qumran Cave is empty now. Perhaps you are feeling empty. What is that about?

- Discover what you need from God now. Ask him to fill your cave.

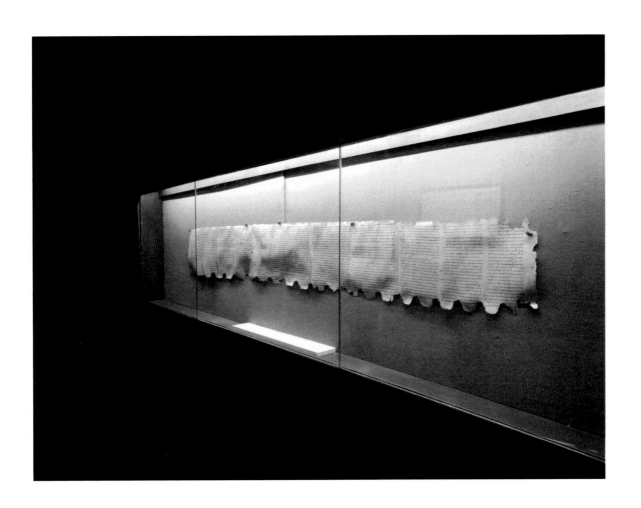

Day 30
A Letter to You from God

Dearest One <u>(your name)</u>,

"When you are afraid, I am with you.
When you feel distressed, I am your God.
I will give you strength and be your helper
With my righteous hand." Is. 41:10

"I know how hard this situation is for you.
I suffered deeply when I became human.
It may difficult to understand why this is happening to you.
For my thoughts and ways are higher than yours."   Is. 55: 8-9.

"Trust me that I will be there with you.
My understanding is endless
I will comfort your weary soul and renew your strength.
We will soar together across the sky like eagles!" Is. 40: 28-31

"I want you to forget the past.
Do not dwell on it anymore.
You are a different person today.
I have forgiven you." Is.43:18

"I will send you a Wonderful Counselor,
A Mighty God,
An Everlasting Father, not like your earthly father.
Your Prince of peace!"   Is. 9:6

"When you go through the fire, you will not burn.
I will be water to your soul.
"When you go through the waters, you will not drown.
I will breathe for you." Is. 43: 2

"You are precious to me." Is. 43: 4

I Love you more than you know!

Papa God

Day 31
The Dead Sea

Due to the high levels of salt, there is no sea life in the Dead Sea; therefore, giving the sea its name. The Dead Sea is a salt lake bordered by Jordan and Israel and is roughly 1,300ft. below sea level. Nearby are the Qumran caves where the Dead Sea Scrolls were found.

Today, people come to enjoy the buoyancy and healing components of the saltwater. Covering our bodies in mud before entering the sea was a way of cleansing our skin. Initially, it felt awkward to maneuver through the dense saltwater, until I decided to let go and just relax. That was truly a unique experience.

Mike Quinn, lead pastor of Newbreak Church, gave a beautiful sermon on healthy self-care. He used an illustration of two buckets, one empty and one full of water, and a dry, cracked sponge. Dipping it into the water, the sponge immediately became plump, and then he poured it into the empty bucket. He said when our sponge is dry, we cannot pour into others. In order to give our time, energy and service to others, we need to take care of ourselves. Another analogy is when the flight attendant asks the parent to put on their oxygen mask first and then their child's mask. Practicing healthy self-care is a way of loving ourselves.

Spiritual Exercise: Self-Care

- Do you believe in taking care of yourself? Why or why not?

- How do you relate to filling your sponge first or putting on your oxygen mask first?

- Are you feeling overly tired, stressed, burnt out? Ask yourself what this is about.

- Draw three circles on a piece of paper, overlapping and connecting them. Label one Spiritual, one Emotional and the other Physical. Write in these circles how you take care of yourself physically, emotionally, and spiritually. Or you may want to draw ways you take care of yourself.

- What nurtures you?

- What drains you?

- Take a look at what you drew in your circles.
  How can you be more balanced?   What do you need to change/add, and what do you need to delete?

- What is at least one thing you can do each day to love yourself?

Day 32
Masada

Here are the ruins of Masada, an ancient city that lies on top of an isolated rock plateau, 1,300 feet high, and became a place where Herod the Great built a fortress for himself. After Herod died in 4BC, the Roman army took it over as an outpost. In 66AD, a group of Jewish rebels overcame the Roman garrison and occupied Masada. Since the Romans were at war, they put aside fighting the rebels until it was over.

When the war finished in 72AD, the Roman army decided to arrest the rebels. It took about a year to build a huge ramp up to the city. You can see a modern ramp in the bottom photo. When they finally breached the wall in 73AD, the Romans found that all 900 Jewish rebels, including women and children, were dead. They had committed suicide by slitting their throats, choosing to die rather than be tortured, raped, and crucified by the Romans. The Jewish historian, Josephus, tells us that two women and five children survived. We don't know if they hid or how long they survived after being captured. But we do have their story.

Reflection

- What speaks to you about this story?

- What do you think of the choice the rebels made?

Day 33
Jerusalem

The top photo, taken at the Israel Museum, is a replica of what Jerusalem looked like in 60 AD. My husband felt that viewing the model from the outside helped him gain perspective on the relative locations we had seen. The bottom photo is of Jerusalem today.

Jerusalem is one of the oldest cities in the world and is considered a holy place to three religions: Judaism, Islam, and Christianity. According to Wikipedia, during its long history, Jerusalem has been destroyed at least twice, besieged 23 times, captured and recaptured 44 times, and attacked 52 times. The excavated City of David, which you will see a photo of, shows the first signs of settlement in the fourth millennium BC.

Both Israel and Palestine have claimed Jerusalem as their capital city. Because of these strong tensions, bloody battles to control the city and sites within have been occurring for thousands of years. While we were there, three young Jewish seminary students were abducted. A massive search started, filling the streets with Israeli soldiers carrying machine guns. We felt safe to continue our travels while hoping for the safe return of these young men. I don't remember exactly how long, but within weeks, they were found dead. They had been tortured and murdered for their faith. I felt heartbroken and deeply disturbed by this terrible injustice.

The Old City is home to several sites of key religious importance: The Temple Mount and Western Wall for Jews, the Church of the Holy Sepulchre for Christians and the Dome of the Rock and al-Aqsa Mosque for Muslims. Today, the Old City is roughly divided into the Muslim, Catholic, Armenian and Jewish Quarters. You can find shops, food, and ancient excavations in each quarter as we continue together on this pilgrimage.

Spiritual Exercise:

- Perhaps today is a day of rest or *Shabbat*. You may want to review your pilgrimage so far, reflecting on what has touched your heart the most. Spend some time in gratitude with God for all you have experienced with him thus far.

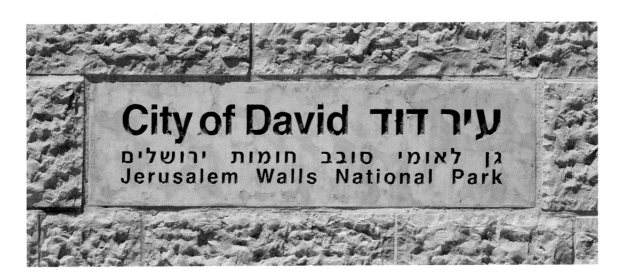

Day 34
The City of David

David (907 BC- 837 BC) was the greatest king of Israel and is still highly revered today. He is my favorite person in the Old Testament. I admire his courage, strength, and boldness as he fought Goliath and won many battles during his time. He deeply loved God and did what was right in his eyes, except for plotting murder against Uriah the Hitite (1 King 15:5). When confronted, he repented, accepted the consequence of his behavior, and received forgiveness and reconciliation from God. Although flawed like we all are, David genuinely desired to do God's will. Scripture tells us that God loved him, saying he was a man after his heart (Acts 13:22).

What moves me the most about David is that he was authentic. He expressed both emotions in the Psalms, both praises along with laments. Some of his beautiful praises have evolved into songs of worship, sung in many churches today. He also mourned over his own failures, expressed hatred for his enemies, and wrestled with God over life's struggles. Authentically, from-the-gut, David wrote these laments without editing his mouth. God not only heard him, He allowed these to be published in his Holy Book. God gives us permission to struggle with him. He is a big God and can take it, knowing that it is for our good to *release* our anger, wailing, and grief.

If David can lament, so can I, and so can you.

Spiritual Exercise: Writing a Lament

How long, LORD? Will you forget me forever? How long will you hide your face from me? How long must I wrestle with my thoughts and day after day have sorrow in my heart? How long will my enemy triumph over me?
Look on me and answer, LORD my God. Give light to my eyes, or I will sleep in death, and my enemy will say, "I have overcome him," and my foes will rejoice when I fall.
But I trust in your unfailing love; my heart rejoices in your salvation.
I will sing the LORD's praise, for he has been good to me. Psalm. 13:1-6.

Haul my betrayers off alive to hell—let them
experience the horror, let them feel every desolate detail of a damned life. Psalm 55:15 MSG

These intense expressions of anger come from a man after God's heart. Deep down, I do not wish ill will on my "enemies," but I have felt intense anger as David did. Growing up, I learned anger was bad. Now I know it is a human emotion, and I'm grateful I can freely express mine to God as David did.

- If you need to mourn, wail, express remorse, or anger towards someone who has wounded you, then write your own lament to God. Try not to edit or judge it. Just let your true feelings out. Remember, God can take it and desires you to be authentic.

Day 35
Psalm 139

Scripture Reflection: Psalm 139

Psalm 139 is one of my favorite psalms. While I have chosen sections of it for a reflection, you may choose to read the entire psalm. Read each section slowly several times.

You have searched me, LORD, and you know me.
You know when I sit and when I rise; you perceive my thoughts from afar. You discern my going out and my lying down; you are familiar with all my ways. Before a word is on my tongue, you, LORD, know it completely. Vs. 1-4

- **How do you feel that God knows you this intimately?**

Where can I go from your Spirit? Where can I flee from your presence? If I go up to the heavens, you are there; if I make my bed in the depths, you are there. Vs. 7-8

- **How do you feel that God is with you *always and everywhere?***

For you created my inmost being; you knit me together in my mother's womb.
I praise you because I am fearfully and wonderfully made; your works are wonderful; I know that full well. Vs. 13-14

- **Write down 20 characteristics about you. List your talents and positive personality traits. Ruminate and meditate on these truths, celebrating how God has uniquely created you.**

How precious to me are your thoughts, God! How vast is the sum of them! Vs.17

- **Write down 20 characteristics about God that are precious to you. Meditate on these.**

Search me, God, and know my heart; test me and know my anxious thoughts. See if there is any offensive way in me and lead me in the way everlasting. Vs. 23-24

- **Daily Prayer of Examen (St. Ignatius of Loyola)**
  - Review your day, either at night or in the morning, reflecting on the previous day.
  - Express gratitude and praises to God for the gifts you received today.
  - What anxious (or other) feelings do you have? Ask: What is that about?
  - Confess any wrongdoing or an offensive way (e.g., hatred) in your heart.
  - Ask God to lead you tomorrow to the way everlasting, to help you release those anxious thoughts and offensive ways.

Day 36
David and Goliath

This photo shows the valley where David slew Goliath, as told in 1 Samuel 17. I did not go there; however, my friend, Irene, did. The Israelites were at war with the Philistines. Sitting on top of the mountain ridge, the Philistine army looked down upon the Israelites below. Sending their strongest warrior, Goliath the giant, the Philistines challenged the Israelites to send one of their soldiers to fight him. Whoever won, the whole army would win.

David was the youngest of Jesse's eight sons, a teenager and a shepherd. He brought food to his brothers, who were out in this field that day. Critical words flew out of his older brother's mouth, ordering David to go back to the sheep. Since the disgusting words coming from Goliath's mouth infuriated David, he ignored his brother. David was strong, emotionally mature, courageous and confident completely in God. Hearing Goliath's challenge, David decided to take him on.

Goliath had height, weight, years of training, full armor, and years of battle experience over David. But David had faith in God. Even though he was a teenager, with no training, no swords, he had experienced great strength as a shepherd by killing lions and bears with his bare hands. When he faced Goliath, he knew that God, who helped him kill the animals, would help him kill this enemy. And that is exactly what happened.

Scripture Reflection

- Read the story of David and Goliath in 1 Samuel 17.

- What speaks to you most about this story?

- Where in your life do you need strength, faith, and courage like David?

- Like David's brothers, who are the critics in your life?

- What or who are the "giants" or obstacles in your life you need to overcome?

- What or who is holding you back?

- What steps can you take to slay your "giant" obstacle?

- Reflect on a time in the past where God helped you "slay an obstacle." Trust him with your current situation.

- Whatever you are facing, ask God to give you courage and strength, as he did David long ago.

Day 37
The Cardo Maximus

The top photo is a painting of the Cardo Maximus or central marketplace for Jerusalem in the 6th Century. This main street was roughly 40 feet wide, lined with Roman era columns on both sides, equivalent to a 4-lane highway today and ran all the way through town, serving both those who lived there and those who traveled from afar.

What you see in the bottom photo are the remains of a portion of the Cardo. These columns supported a roof that covered the area, protecting the shoppers from the sun and rain.

Visio Divina

- Spend some time gazing at the photos above.

- What do you notice?

- What do you need to shop for now? In other words, what do you need from God now?

- As the roof protected the shoppers form sun and rain, what do you need to have God protect you from?

- Write your insights and wisdom received from God in your journal.

Day 38
Market Place Today

Seeing this man selling bread reminded me of that famous Al-Anon quote:

"Don't go into the hardware store expecting to buy bread."

This tool has been life changing for me in my relationships. If I desire nourishment from bread (e.g. encouragement), I cannot expect that from a hardware store. I can buy a hammer which is very good and useful for building structures and hanging pictures. However, a hammer does not provide the emotional support I need. If I want bread, or encouragement, I can to go to the bakery. In other words, I seek to get the encouragement I need from someone else or someplace else that can offer it. And here is the key: not to beat myself up because I didn't get bread or encouragement from that hardware store, and not to beat up the hardware store--for that is who he or she is, and that is what they are able to offer. I tell myself that I am okay, and the hardware store (i.e. a person in my life) is okay. We are both works in progress and children of God. We can't expect another human being to fulfill all our needs. I have learned over time to surrender my unrealistic expectations to God. Most of all, I get the encouragement and love I desire from God because his love is the only love that truly satisfies.

In your journal answer the following questions:

- Name someone you want a better relationship with.
- What do you want from them? Be honest and don't judge your desires.
- Are your expectations realistic or unrealistic?
- What need is this person able to meet? Maybe the hardware store can't give you encouragement but he or she can give you tools.
- What are your deeper needs in this relationship? (security, significance, respect, to be loved, heard, or valued, etc.)
- Are you able to talk to this person about your needs and expectations?
- How do you feel when you can't meet someone's expectations of you?

When you are ready, sit with God in silence.

- Breathe in and out slowly.
- Offer yourself compassion for not receiving what you need. Then offer the other person compassion for not being able to give that to you.
- Breathe in *I am your Beloved,* breathe out *he or she is Your beloved.* Breathe in *I am okay,* breathe out *he or she is okay.* Repeat this until you feel peace inside.
- Slowly let go and release your expectations to God.
- Ask God to for the right person to meet your needs and allow him to meet your deepest needs.

Day 39
The Western Wall

The Western Wall or Wailing Wall is located in the old City of Jerusalem and is the only remains of the second temple of Jerusalem, which was destroyed by the Romans in 70 AD. This wall is considered sacred and a place of prayer for Jews, Christians, and pilgrims. The area is divided into two parts, one for men and one for women. What you see here is the women's side. My guide told me that men and women are separated so the men will not be distracted by seeing an attractive woman.

I felt so grateful to be in this sacred place, writing my prayers on a small piece of paper. The distraction of the crowds melted away as I pressed into the presence of God.

- What distracts you from praying or talking to God?

This photo is the women's side of the wall. Many people come and write their prayer requests and put them in the crevices of the wall. Our guide told us that when the crevices are overflowing with requests, someone gathers the papers, treats them as sacred, and buries them. They are not burned or thrown away like trash. Even these thousands of tiny papers were considered precious and sacred. Although some of our prayers remain unanswered, I believe that God holds them as sacred, not ignoring or throwing them away like trash.

- What prayers are written on your slip of paper?

Day 40
The Steps Leading to the Temple Mount

Here you see an enormous flight of steps, excavated in 1967, that led to the southern wall of the Temple Mount. I spent some time going up and down each step, some original and some restored, wondering if Jesus did the same in this exact place. Just to be the area where Jesus walked was a long-awaited dream of mine.

Long ago, The Temple was where the Israelites offered animal sacrifices for their sins. Christians believe that Jesus was the ultimate sacrifice. The Apostle Paul talked in Romans 12: 1-2 about offering our bodies, our whole being, as a living sacrifice to God. Here is what he says:

"So, here's what I want you to do, God helping you: Take your everyday, ordinary life—your sleeping, eating, going to work, and walking around life—and place it before God as an offering. Embracing what God does for you is the best thing you can do for him. Don't become so well adjusted to your culture that you fit into it without even thinking. Instead, fix your attention on God. You'll be changed from the inside out. Readily recognize what he wants from you, and quickly respond to it. Unlike the culture around you, always dragging you down to its level of immaturity, God brings the best out of you, develops well-formed maturity in you."
Romans 12: 1-2 MSG

Spiritual Exercise

- Make a list of your everyday life activities.

- Ask yourself: How can I experience God in _____?

  Here are some examples:

  -When cooking, see what new ingredients you need in your life (e.g. patience, joy) and what ingredients do you need to leave out (e.g., negativity, complaining).

  -Gardening; ask what needs to be pruned in order to grow or what is beautiful in your life.

  -Driving in the car; turn the radio off and talk to God as if he is in the sit next to you.

Day 41
Mikvah

Ancient Mikvahs, like this one, have been discovered and excavated all over Israel. In Judaism, ritual washing, or ablution, happens by immersing the whole body in a Mikveh. This was a way of purifying their soul, particularly before entering the temple and offering sacrifices to God. The belief is that the cleansing prepares the person to face God, life, and people with a fresh spirit and new eyes, washing away the past, leaving only the future. Other reasons for ceremonial washing include women to cleanse after menstruation or childbirth, for anyone who had been in contact with the ill, certain rules pertaining to animal sacrifices, and to immerse a corpse before burial. Today, Orthodox Jews still use a Mikvah for ritual purifications for most of the same reasons as long ago. A few more reasons include: a bride and bridegroom cleansing before their wedding night, a new convert, new eating utensils and dishes, and honoring Jewish holidays. Some funeral homes have their own mikveh to cleanse the body before burial.

I was inspired to take a warm bath and turn it into a ritual. Laying in the tub, submerged in the warm water, was like feeling God's extravagant love surrounding my whole being. Slowly lathering my skin with soap, I imagined washing away anything that keeps me from believing that I am his beloved daughter. Then I asked what needs to be made clean in me so I can see God and other people with a new freshness.

I want to see people as unique with both talents and flaws, works in progress, and beloved children of God.

Spiritual Exercise

- Imagine that the warm water of the shower flowing over your body is God's extravagant love pouring out on you. Feel the pleasure this brings.

- Take a shower or bath, and imagine God cleansing your soul as you wash your body. What do you need him to cleanse, so your eyes will see God, life, and yourself with new freshness?

Day 42
The Golden Menorah

Here is the Golden Menorah, modeled after the menorah in the temple long ago. Described in the Bible as the seven-lamp ancient Hebrew lampstand made of pure gold, the menorah was used in the portable sanctuary set up by Moses in the wilderness and later in the Temple in Jerusalem. Fresh olive oil of the purest quality was burned daily to light its lamps. The menorah has been a symbol of Judaism since ancient times and is a reminder of the seven days of Creation.

Scripture Reflection or Creative Art

Read Genesis Chapters one and two. Here is a summary with suggestions for each day. You may choose to draw or paint each day.

- Day 1: *God created the heavens and the earth, both day and night.*
  What does this say to you about God?

- Day 2: *God created the sky and atmospheres surrounding the earth.*
  Lay down in your yard and gaze at the sky or the clouds. Breathe in the air. What do the air and the sky tell you about God?

- Day 3: *God created land, waters, and plants.*
  Take a walk out in nature or sit in your backyard. Notice the many different kinds of trees and plants there are. What does this say to you about God?

- Day 4: *God created the sun, stars, and moon.*
  Lay out in your backyard at night. Gaze at the stars on a clear night and the moon if it is visible. How does this speak to you about God?

- Day 5: *God created all the creatures of the sea, the birds and the bugs.*
  What does God say to you through the fish in the sea? The birds in the air? And the bugs, although often not welcomed, they do have a purpose.

- Day 6: *God created all the animals. He also created man in his image.*
  Spend time with your pet, if you have one. How do you experience God's love or pleasure? Take some time and look at your body, how exquisite and intricately it is formed in God's image. And it is good! How does this speak to you?

- Day 7: *God rested.*
  And he was God! Take time to rest.

Day 43
Oil Lamps

This really caught my eye, as there are many references in scripture about oil lamps. I wondered what it was like to have these small lamps as the main source of light after sundown. I felt so grateful for electricity.

I was reminded of the times God has been my light, my guide throughout my life. And I desire to be a light for him. Like a small flame lights up a darkened room, so does our light of God's love to a darkened world. Even the smallest flame has value. Let your light shine!

Scripture Reflection

Thy word is a lamp unto my feet, and a light unto my path. Psalm 119:105

- Say the scripture out loud three times.

- What scriptures are a lamp unto your feet?

- Reflect on a time when God was a light for your path.

- How are you a light for God?

- What is your invitation?

Day 44
Pool of Siloam

In this photo, you see the steps that lead down into The Pool of Siloam. Where there is grass and shrubs on the left was once filled with water. The Pool of Siloam was a rock-cut pool on the southern slope of the City of David and fed by the waters of the Gihon Spring, carried there by two aqueducts. People believed the pool had special healing power and is mentioned in Nehemiah 3:15 and John 9:1.

The story of the blind man from birth is told in John 9:1. Believing that sin caused illness, the people asked Jesus who sinned, the man's parents or himself? Jesus replied neither. He healed the man, giving him eyes to see.

As I sat here, reflecting on the healing of the blind man, I thought of the hurtful things people say to those who are suffering. Previously, I mentioned a friend of ours, Ted, who has ALS. He is such a good man with a great heart. Again, someone in the church accused him of not tithing a full 10%, so this is why he got ALS. I felt like slapping that man.

Long ago, people asked Jesus if this blind man sinned or his parents did, causing the blindness. Jesus told them neither. And I say the same.

Reflection

- Reflect on a time you were suffering, either from emotional or physical pain. Make a list of some helpful things people said to you. How did that make you feel?

- What were the not so helpful or hurtful things people said to you? Write those down. How did that make you feel?

- What were some intentional or unintentional hurtful things you have said?

- Offer forgiveness and compassion to others and yourself.

Before I received my training, I told a friend who lost a sibling in a car accident that his loved one is now in heaven. Not the right thing to say. I apologized and felt so grateful when he forgave the ignorant: me.

Prayer: Forgiving the Ignorant

Like Jesus prayed on the cross, *Father, forgive them for they know not what they do.*

Pray: *Father, forgive _____ for they know not what they say.*

Day 45
The Eastern Gate

The Eastern Gate is also known as the Golden Gate or Beautiful Gate. Being the oldest gate in the Old City, it was built around 520 AD. The original gate was destroyed by the Romans around 70 AD and is where Jesus went in and out of the city many times, including the triumphant entry on Palm Sunday. Judaism teaches that the Messiah will enter through this gate. A Muslim ruler during medieval times had the gate walled up and placed a cemetery in front. Christians believe The Messiah, Jesus, has already fulfilled this prophecy.

Standing on the top of the Mount of Olives, I could see this gate and imagine what that triumphant day was like. A crown gathering, laying their cloaks down for Jesus as he rode on a donkey through town. Waving palm branches, shouting joyfully, "Hosanna! Hosanna!"

What I noticed was that Jesus did not get *hooked* into the praises by men. I assume he liked it as most of us do, yet he chose not to let it go to his head. He kept going, even though within a few days, the sounds of "Hosanna!" would soon shift into "Crucify!" Jesus did not get *hooked* into the "Crucifys" either. He probably felt very hurt by the cruel words from the crowds and mocking by the soldiers, and yet that didn't shake his identity. His ego did not inflate when hearing praise nor deflate when hearing damnation. Jesus was grounded as the Beloved of God and knew what he was called to do.

Scripture Reflection

- The Triumphant entry is in all four gospels (Matthew 21:1-17, Mark 11:1-11, Luke 19:29-40, John 12:12-19). Choose a passage or read all four.

- What is God saying to you through this story?

- Most of us like it when people say good things about us and feel hurt when people say bad things about us. The more we are grounded in our identity, the easier we will not be "swayed" from our purpose or get "hooked" into the praises or criticisms of other people.

What speaks to you about this?

Day 46
The Upper Room

The "Upper Room" is in the David's Tomb Compound in Jerusalem and is believed to be the site of the Last Supper. In Christian tradition, the room was not only the site of the Last Supper but also where the Holy Spirit alighted upon the apostles and other believers at Pentecost. It is sometimes thought to be the place where the apostles stayed in Jerusalem. Today, a modern room has replaced the original room of long ago.

I reflected on the passage in John 13, where Jesus washes the disciples' feet that night of the Last Supper in the Upper Room. In those days, with walking the main form of transportation and wearing only sandals, feet were tired, dirty, smelly, and sore. Foot washing was also a sign of cleansing one's soul and often done by a servant. Here Jesus performs a tremendous act of humility and love. He is their (and our) role model not to think of ourselves too highly but to humble ourselves, genuinely desiring God's best for others. And he even did this to Peter, who would soon deny him, and to Judas who would betray him to the authorities. *That is genuine, selfless love.*

Several years ago, I watched my daughter, Katie, rub my mother-in-law's feet as she laid in the hospital bed. Such compassion she offered, without drawing attention to herself. This brought tears to my eyes.

Spiritual Exercise

- Treat yourself to a pedicure. As your feet are being washed and massaged, close your eyes, sink into the chair and imagine Jesus is doing this to you. Allow yourself to feel both physical and emotional pleasure.

- Think of a situation where you can humbly offer an act of kindness to someone in your life.

- Partake in communion either at church or with a community of believers. Use this time to reflect on The Last Supper.

Day 47
The Garden of Gethsemane

Here is a photo of the Garden of Gethsemane filled with olive trees, some being 100 years old. My tour guide couldn't believe it when the crowds suddenly dispersed, and we were one of the few people remaining in the garden. Again, I knew in my heart that God made the way for me to be quiet, still, and just sit in this sacred place. I had an hour to just sit and contemplate alone over that dreadful night. I was deeply moved by being in the Garden of Gethsemane, where Jesus prayed in agony the night before he was arrested. Jesus felt all the emotions we have felt. He even struggled with God, which gives us permission to struggle with him. After Jesus pleaded his heart out for the cup to be taken away, he chose God's will over his own. I wrote this adaptation from Mark 14:32-50, on how Jesus felt.

"After our last supper together, I took my disciples to Gethsemane. I asked them to sit for a while and keep watch with me while I prayed. Slowly, I wandered over to a large rock. Suddenly, I became deeply distressed and troubled. My soul was overwhelmed, full of sorrow to the point of death.

My knees collapsed as I fell to the ground. 'I don't think I can do this,' crying out to my Father to take this cup away from me. The thought of crucifixion was more than I could bear. Being whipped and beaten, then having my flesh torn away from the nails, hanging on that tree while I slowly suffocate with each breath. *Please, God*, let there be another way, I begged, wrestling with him.

Then I turned to my best friends, and they were asleep. I nudged Peter and asked him if he could just stay awake with me for an hour. The spirit is willing, but the body is weak. Please come be with me. I really need you now.

Returning to prayer, I implored God again to take this cup away. Balls of sweat streamed down my face. Wiping it away, I saw it was blood. Feeling devastated, I turned to my friends for support, and they were asleep again! Startled, they woke and stared at me with those heavy eyelids. They didn't know what to say to me. My heart was pulverized.

I continued to pray, beseeching God one last time to take the cup away. After several minutes, I could feel my whole being surrender. Finally, I told him *Not my will, but Thine.* Somehow, I knew deep in my soul that I would get through this. And like my Father, I so loved everyone in the world, wishing none would perish, but live eternally in heaven. I desired to do this, no matter the cost.

Returning to my disciples, I couldn't believe they were sleeping again. Anger boiled within me as I shouted, "Enough! Get up. The hour has come. Rise. Let's go. Here comes my betrayer!"

Then Judas arrived with a crowd, carrying clubs and swords. Are you kidding me? They know I am not rebellious and violent. Then he had the gall to betray me with a kiss. It broke my heart that this man was once a close friend, but greed overtook his soul.

Then my best friends all fled, deserting me in my greatest hour of need. I felt so abandoned. As the soldiers led me away, I could feel God assuring me that the outcome will be glorious, and he will be with me…in the pain…all the way to the end."

Here is a photo of the rock, inside the Church of Gethsemane, which some believe is the rock Jesus prayed in agony over. Many come and kneel, touching the rock, as they pray to God.

Imaginative Prayer

- Read the scripture slowly, as told in Mark 14:32-50.

- Take a few minutes to relax in your chair. Breathe deeply. You can close your eyes or focus on one of the photos.

- Now imagine you are in the garden. You are watching this scene. What do you see? Smell? Hear? What does the garden look like?

- Now you see Jesus, in agony, praying. How do you feel?

- Is there someone who has betrayed, hurt or abandoned you? Talk to Jesus about this.

- Are you in a circumstance that you are angry about? Talk to Jesus about it, expressing how you honestly feel about the experience.

- Give yourself permission to wrestle with God. Ask to take the cup away.

- Now Jesus invites you to join him in the pain.
  Sit with him and allow him to enter into your pain.

- When you are ready, pray: *Not my will, but Thine.*

Day 48
Caiaphas' House

In this photo are the original steps leading up to the house of Caiaphas. Jesus actually walked up these steps after his arrest, and this is also where Peter denied him three times. Inside the house is where Jesus was first interrogated after his arrest. Joseph ben Caiaphas, a Jewish high priest in 18-36 AD, organized a plot to kill Jesus and then presided over the Sanhedrin trial. The primary sources for Caiaphas' life are in the writings of Josephus and the New Testament (Matthew 26:57-75). Mark 14:62 tells us that Caiaphas and the other men charged him with blasphemy and sentenced him to corporal punishment for his crime.

> *Those who had seized Jesus led him away to Caiaphas, the high priest, where the scribes and the elders were gathered together.* Matt. 26:57

We did not visit Caiaphas' house, but my friend Irene did. Here is what she said about this place:

> "We descended into the dungeon. The area is well lit now, but I could only imagine how dark and dank it must have been. It is here in the prison that Jesus was beaten. Possibly flogged with canes. Unlike depictions I had of Jesus tied to a post, a prisoner was tied with hands and feet spread apart, a foot off the ground. Just the suspended position is painful to contemplate and then to receive the decreed beating, a brutal scene. It was suspected that Jesus would not survive the night, but he did and in the morning was then taken to Pilate."

Reflection

- Have you ever been falsely accused of something you didn't do or received undeserved punishment? What happened?

- How did that make you feel?

- Where are you in the process of healing from this injustice?

- Perhaps you have witnessed an injustice to someone else. How does this make you feel?

- Are you called to any action towards social justice?

- Sit with Jesus in the prison for a while. He does understand your pain, even though God didn't cause his and didn't cause yours.

Day 49
The Crown of Thorns

...and then twisted together a crown of thorns and set it on his head. They put a staff in his right hand. Then they knelt in front of him and mocked him. "Hail, king of the Jews!" they said.
Matt. 27:29

Visio Divina

- Spend some time gazing at this photo.

- What do you notice?

- What stirs inside of you?

- What is God saying to you through this photo?

Day 50
Via Dolorosa

As we began the Via Dolorosa, you can see what looks like a cross on the street from the sun's reflection. I felt such joy and sadness at the same time. The way Jesus suffered tremendously is beyond my comprehension. And yet joy for his extravagant love so I can have a deep relationship with him here, now and forever.

This next section of photos will be of the Via Dolorosa or Stations of the Cross. I have a few photos for some of the stations. You may want to search for a print or use your imagination to picture what happened for those stations without photos.

Stations ten through fourteen are inside the Church of the Holy Sepulchre, which is considered one of the holiest Christian sites, being the place where many believe Jesus was crucified and buried. Others believe the crucifixion and resurrection happened in the location of the Garden Tomb, which you will see later.

God blessed me again by creating some space for me to be alone. In several of the small chapels, I was the only one. Inside the Church of the Holy Sepulchre, my guide said he had never seen it so sparse. He said he usually has to wait a very long time on the steps leading up to the last stations. We climbed right up. Then he tried to discourage me from waiting an hour or more to enter the shrine (Station XIV) that holds the tomb of Jesus. My daughters complained about standing in line. I looked at them and said, "You have stood in line for an hour to get on a ride at Disneyland, you can wait in this line, too." I had gone this far and wanted to finish it, so I ignored my guide and my daughters and got in line. Ten minutes is all we waited. Again, my grateful heart rejoiced at God's precious gift to me.

I encourage you to take your time through these stations. Use whatever practice you choose. Or just let the photo or station speak to you. I will have a brief prayer at each station.

Prayer: *Lord, open my eyes, my mind, and my heart as I enter the way of the cross. May I have no expectations but only to deepen my relationship with you.*

I. Jesus is condemned to death

Prayer: *Lord, I can't imagine the sorrow you felt for being falsely condemned.
I am grateful I am no longer condemned for _____ since your Holy Spirit
lives in me.*

II. Jesus receives his cross

Prayer: *A heavy cross is shoved upon you.*
Lord, help me receive this cross of_____ that I have been given in life.

III. Jesus falls the first time under his cross

Prayer: *Lord, the weight of this cross crushed your broken body.*
I remember that time when I felt _____ was pushing me down. Please help
me the next time I fall.

IV. Jesus meets his mother

Prayer: *Lord, the pain in your mother's eyes is beyond words.*
I express gratitude to my mother for _____ and I forgive her for _____.

V. Simon of Cyrene helps Jesus to carry his cross

Prayer: *Lord, your Father provided someone to help you carry your burden.*
I am grateful to _____ for coming alongside me when I was in dire need.
May I come alongside _____ in their time of dire need.

VI. Veronica wipes the face of Jesus

Prayer: *The blood from the crown of thorns, flowed down your face.*
Lord, please wipe away my _____ so I may be a light for you.

VII. Jesus falls for the second time

Prayer: *Lord, the pain you felt as your body crashes to the ground.*
This weight of _____ that I am carrying now is so much to bear.
May your strength help me get back up.

VIII. Jesus speaks to the women of Jerusalem

Prayer: *Lord, I truly admire how even through tremendous suffering, you still encouraged others.*
Lord, even when times are difficult for me, help me speak encouraging words to
_____ just as you did to the women of Jerusalem long ago.

IX. Jesus falls for the third time

Prayer: *Lord, your weakened body can carry no more.*
Lord, carry me in _____ when I can bear it no more.

X. Jesus is stripped of his garments

Prayer: *Lord, how humiliating this must have felt for you.*
Please heal me of my shame from _____ that I feel now.

XI. Jesus is nailed to the cross

Prayer: *Lord, I can't imagine the pain of those nails tearing into your flesh.*
Help me let go of that painful event _____ that ripped my heart.

XII. Jesus dies on the cross

Silence

XIII. Jesus is taken down from the cross

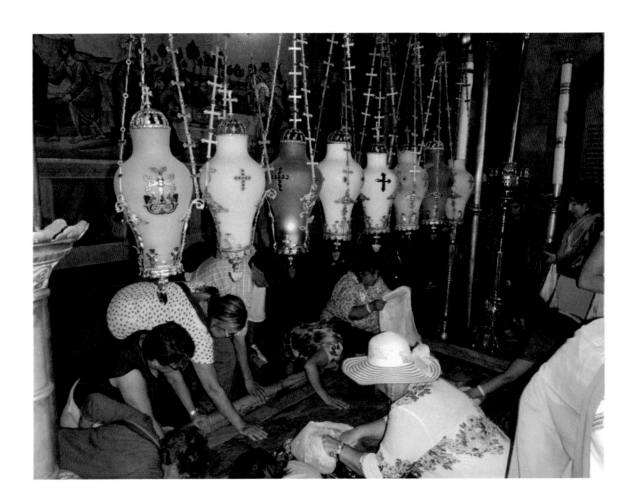

Prayer: *Lord, God provided for you even in death. As Joseph of Arimathea and Nicodemus carried your body from the cross to a slab of stone, please carry me when _____ for I have nothing left to give. May I be reminded to do the same for _____.*

XIV. Jesus is laid in the tomb

Prayer: *Lord, I take time to grieve over the losses in my life of dreams, unanswered prayers, hopes, health, wealth or _____.*

Prayer: *Lord, I grieve over the loss of the relationships in my life* _____
_____ *whether through distance, separation, discord,*
or death.

Day 51
Grief

After I finished the Via Dolorosa, I took a few moments to reflect on what God was inviting me into. One invitation is to not be afraid when I am faced with suffering and death. God brought Jesus support along the way, some who he barely knew. Veronica wiped his face. Simon of Cyrene helped carry his cross. Joseph of Arimathea offered his family tomb and carried Jesus' body along with Nicodemus, who was a secret follower. A few of his closest loved ones were there; his mother, Mary Magdalene, and John however, the rest of his family were not, and neither were his disciples. But God met his needs, so he didn't face death alone.

I recalled when my mother died, a person I barely knew showed up on my doorstep with dinner. I was so grateful for this surprise gift at a much-needed time. Like God took care of his son, he took care of me, too.

Spiritual Practice: Grief

Sit in quiet with God. Ask yourself *what did I miss out on? What or who have I lost?* In your journal or on a piece of paper, write your list. Examples:

Loss of a dream   Loss of health

Loss of job or career path   Unmet desires

Loss of a healthy childhood   Unanswered prayer

Loss of material possessions   Loss of a trophy or prize

Loss of relationship through death, conflict, or drifting apart

Loss of loving family members, relatives, clergy, teachers, etc.

- Whatever it is, take some time and allow yourself to grieve. Grief comes and goes. No two people grieve the same. Do what works for you, not what other people tell you do.

- Allow the feelings (sadness, disappointment, hurt, regrets, etc.) to happen and just sit with them. Try not to end this time too quickly. Invite Jesus to sit with you.

- Receive compassion from God. Offer yourself compassion.

Day 52
Golgotha

Although some scholars believe that Jesus was crucified in the Church of the Holy Sepulchre, others believe it happened here. Scripture says he was crucified at Golgotha, The Skull. You can see that the rock formation does look like a skull. My tour guide said this was the actual place of punishment for thousands of years, so he believed this was where Jesus was crucified. This place was right outside the Damascus gate with a road leading away from the city. For capital punishment, the Jews preferred stoning someone to death while the Romans preferred crucifixion. In order to instill fear for all those entering the city, the crosses were lined up along the road, with rotting bodies left for days. He also told me that the condemned were stripped naked to humiliate them. They did not carry the whole cross, only the horizontal, as the vertical post or tree was already in the ground. Evidence of bones with the nails driven in through the ankles suggest the feet were strapped on either the side of the post. The condemned hung low on the cross, possibly a foot or two from the ground, not high on the cross as depicted in paintings. Jesus did utter a few things as he hung on the cross. If he were high up, the people would not have heard him. Now today, this place is for buses to park.

Gazing at the Skull, a chill ran down my spine. A strong sensation told me that this was indeed the place where Jesus was crucified. I chose to sit and reflect on Jesus' last seven utterances.

Scripture Reflection: Seven Utterances of Christ on the Cross

"Father, forgive them; for they do not know what they are doing." Luke 23:34
Who do you need to forgive, whether they were intentional or not?

"Truly I say to you, today you shall be with me in Paradise." Luke 23:43
The thief was offered heaven last minute, didn't ask for forgiveness, and didn't earn it by living a perfect life. How does this make you feel?

"Woman, here is your son," and to the disciple, *"Here is your mother."* John 19:26-27
Jesus asks John to take care of his mother, not his brothers and sisters. What are your thoughts about this?

"Eli, Eli, lama sabachthani?" that is, *"My God, My God, why hast Thou forsaken me?"* Matt. 27:46
Jesus' humanity is shown here. When have you felt forsaken by God?

"I am thirsty." John 19:28
What are you thirsty for?

"Father, into Thy hands I commit my spirit." Luke 23:46
What do you need to commit into God's hands?

"It is finished!" John 19:30
What do you want to finish in your life?

Day 53
The Garden Tomb

Here is what some scholars believe is the actual tomb where Jesus was laid. Joseph of Arimathea offered Jesus to be laid in his personal family tomb. In those days, the body was laid in a tomb for a year. After that time, the bones were gathered and placed in a sarcophagus made of stone. Joseph was a man of wealth who could afford a tomb like this one. According to scripture, Joseph of Arimathea and Nicodemus carried the body from the cross to the tomb, which wouldn't have been far. This tomb is near Golgotha and is in a garden.

We were able to spend time in the garden, reflecting, praying, and taking communion together. Although there are more than just seven phrases Christ spoke after the resurrection, I will share some according to the gospel of John over the next seven days, along with reflection questions or a practice. As David is my favorite in the Old Testament, John is my favorite in the New. He was there at the tomb. Being very close to Jesus, he tells us in his gospel that he was the disciple whom Jesus loved. Not that Jesus didn't love the others, but there was an intimate relationship between the two of them. I also think John really got it, that he was the beloved son of God. My hope is that you will really get this, too.

Spiritual Practice: Joy (By Sheryl Fleisher)[4]

- Name three things that brought you joy today or yesterday.

- Take a few minutes feeling the pleasure and joy these things brought you.

- Invite God into this time with you. Experience joy together.

Day 54

"Mary." John 20:16

Here is a woman, mourning inside the Garden Tomb. Long ago, Mary Magdalene rose early that Sunday morning and found the tomb empty. Already grieving from the loss of her Rabboni (Teacher), she is filled with despair that the body is missing. Not recognizing Jesus, thinking he was the gardener, she pleads through her tears as to where he has moved the body. Then Jesus lovingly says her name, *"Mary."*

I was reminded of something powerful I learned at supervision training for spiritual directors:

"Stop grave digging. There is only decay and bones there."
Father Joe McHugh

Grave digging is different than mourning over loss, with the latter being a healthy process. Grave digging is beating ourselves up for our past mistakes. Rehearsing that video in our heads is like a decaying stench to our soul. Once we have received forgiveness and forgiven ourselves, then it is time to leave it behind and go to the place that gives life.

Reflection

- How do you feel when Jesus lovingly calls your name?

- If you are mourning, allow yourself to be comforted by Jesus.

- If you are a grave digging, look at the video playing in your head. Is there something that needs to be processed or forgiven? If not, take the video out and throw it away.

- Jesus is not at the grave anymore. Why are you?

Day 55

"Peace be with you." John 20:19

Reflection

- As you gaze at the picture, what is speaking to you?

- What peace do you need in your life now?

- What practices help you feel peace?

- Spend time praying for peace for your city, country, and the world.

Day 56

"Put your finger here; see my hands. Reach your hand and put it into my side. Stop doubting and believe." John 20: 27

Thomas was a disciple of Jesus during his three-year ministry. He witnessed the miracles, heard his preaching and experienced his deep friendship. Yet he struggled with doubt. After the resurrection, Thomas stated he would not believe Jesus rose from the dead unless he put his hands in his wounds. Jesus did not criticize him for doubting, nor beat him up for abandoning him at the cross. He did not say, "What's the matter with you? Didn't you witness all those miracles? Don't you remember when I raised Lazarus from the dead?" Instead, he offered his wounds to Thomas. *What a genuine action of love and grace!* Thomas' faith and trust were deepened as a result. Jesus did tell Thomas to stop doubting and believe. Then he went on to say that we (you and me) are truly blessed when we believe, even though we have not seen, have not witnessed. I felt reassured that I could talk to God when I struggle with doubt when things don't work out how I had hoped.

Reflection

- What do you doubt?

- How do these words of Jesus speak to you?

Day 57

"Come and have breakfast." John 21:12

I don't know if Jesus needed to eat with his new transformed body, but he made his disciples breakfast back in Galilee. After all that had happened, he made sure their needs were met, including a simple meal. I was very grateful to eat "St. Peter's fish" here in the photo.

   I practice gratitude every day. Whether it is a small gift, like a piece of dark chocolate, my cat purring as we snuggle, or a kind gesture from a loved one. Neuroscience confirms the benefit in the brain when practicing gratitude. I can feel the positive energy flow through my body and an overall sense of well-being.

Reflection

- What are you hungry for?
- Jesus says to you, *"Come and have_____."*

Spiritual Practice: Gratitude

- At the end of the day, name at least five things that you were grateful for that day. Or in the morning, name five things you were grateful for the previous day.

- Notice the gifts you receive throughout your day and say a breath prayer of gratitude.

- Keep a gratitude journal. This reminds you of all the gifts God has given you.

- Whether big or small, choose gratitude over being negative or resentful of what you do not have.

- Feel how God treasures you as you practice gratitude.

Day 58

"Receive the Holy Spirit." John 20:22

Christians believe that the Holy Spirit of God lives in each of us. Like the air we breathe, we cannot see it but know it's there, filling our lungs with each breath we take. And I trust the air is present always. God desires a faith where we know his Spirit is with us *always,* even when we don't feel it.

According to scripture, the Holy Spirit is our guide, counselor, healer, and comforter. The Spirit gives us wisdom, strength, and power. Communion is a way of receiving the Spirit of Christ.

The fruit of the Holy Spirit is love, joy, peace, patience, kindness, goodness, gentleness, faithfulness and self-control (Galatians 5:22). I am going to add power, wisdom, courage, hope, and internal freedom. As we remain in the Holy Spirit, we can see these fruits in our lives. This is what I believe is the abundant life that Jesus said he came to give us. This kind of life is open to all.

Spiritual Practice: Examen of The Fruit of the Spirit

As you pray, ask God for wisdom. Review the fruit of the Spirit mentioned above. See which one jumps out at you. Ask yourself these questions:

Where did I feel or experience _____ today?

Where did I show or display _____ today?

For example, where did I feel God's love for me today? Perhaps in a smile or a kind word from someone. Or a dog that wags his tail as you walk in the room. Even a simple prayer for someone or sending a kind text can be an act of love.

What blocked me from _____ today? What was that about?

How can I be more _____ tomorrow?

For example, what blocked me from being patient today? Road rage? Or something didn't go my way? Maybe slowing down and trying a few breath prayers while I am driving might help me be more patient in the car.

Take your time. This is a life-long spiritual practice. You may want to go through several fruits or just reflect on one until you start to see a change in your life. The Holy Spirit within you can help you along the way.

Day 59

"Do you love me? Feed my sheep." John 21:17

Jesus went back to Galilee after the resurrection. A deeply moving story is that of Jesus reconciling with Peter, as told by John 21:15-17.

> *¹⁵ When they had finished eating, Jesus said to Simon Peter, "Simon, son of John, do you love me more than these?"*
>
> *"Yes, Lord," he said, "you know that I love you." Jesus said, "Feed my lambs."*
> *¹⁶ Again, Jesus said, "Simon son of John, do you love me?"*
>
> *He answered, "Yes, Lord, you know that I love you." Jesus said, "Take care of my sheep."*
> *¹⁷ The third time, he said to him, "Simon, son of John, do you love me?"*
>
> *Peter was hurt because Jesus asked him the third time, "Do you love me?" He said, "Lord, you know all things; you know that I love you." Jesus said, "Feed my sheep.*

Such a beautiful picture of a deep love, forgiveness, and healing. Here, Jesus does not beat Peter up for denying him, nor hiding in fear after his death. He reaches out to Peter in love, drawing him back into this cherished friendship. Soon, Peter will be empowered by the Holy Spirit, performing many miracles, to share the good news of Christ. Seeing the change from fear to boldness in all the disciples, being willing to die for their faith, convinces me that Jesus is the Divine.

Imaginative Prayer

- Read the passage slowly, letting the words sink in. Look at the photo or close your eyes and imagine the scene. Use your senses.

- Put yourself in the passage as Peter. Jesus looks at you with warmth and love in his eyes. How do you answer Jesus when he asks you if you love him?

- Who are the sheep or lambs you are to feed and take care of?

- Spend some time relishing in this time of reconciliation and love with Jesus.

God truly desires to reconcile with you. No matter what you have done or how you see yourself, he longs to draw you closer into his friendship. *It's never too late.*

Day 60

"Peace be with you! As the Father has sent me, I am sending you." John 20:21

Not only does our spiritual transformation process deepen our relationship with God and ourselves, but also helps us love other people. This may not be a warm fuzzy feeling but a genuine desire to treat others as we want to be treated. We were created for community, to do life with, and come alongside others. God has created each of us unique and gifted with a purpose. As a Spiritual Director and wounded healer, I am honored to come alongside others as they seek to deepen their relationship with God.

- Where is God sending you after this journey? Perhaps to another country? Or out in your community? Or to be with family? Or to just be with him alone on a retreat or sabbatical to refresh?

I want to thank you for coming on this pilgrimage with me. In the introduction, the definition of a pilgrimage is defined as a journey in search of a new or expanded meaning of self, others, and God through the experience. The focus is on gleaming spiritual insights of the places, not so much on obtaining information. The hope is that this pilgrimage will lead to transformation from God after one has returned home, in his or her everyday life.

So, the final reflection questions are:

- Summarize any new, expanding meaning of yourself.

- How have you drawn closer, deeper in your relationship with God?

- What has been transformed in you?

- What is an invitation or call to service for you?

- Spend time expressing gratitude for the insights you have received.

May you know deep within that you are the Beloved of God!

Acknowledgements

I am so grateful for my family who went on this pilgrimage with me. They gave me the time and space I needed. My husband has been a tremendous support with preparing the photos and the formatting of this book.

I appreciate my friend, Irene Anderson, for giving me permission to use her photos of the boat on the Sea of Galilee, Migdal, David and Goliath, Caiaphas' house, and the crown of thorns. And to Domingo Cabrera who gave me permission to use his photo of Jacob's well. Finally, to my dear family, Ron, Shaina, and Katie who took all the remaining photos.

My critique group has been such a blessing to me. I thank Julie Watson, Jeanne Cesena, Corrine LaCroix Rourke, Monica Gaut, and Kamaria Allen, along with my writing partner Beverly Peterson who offered both critique and encouragement.

Regina Shin, RSCJ, gave me advice on how to use and display the photos in this book.

I am grateful to Chou Hallegra, who edited, designed graphics, and helped with the book launch.

My sister, Judy Shubin, spent time proofreading my final copy which was such a valued gift to me.

Most of all, I am grateful to God, who cleared the crowds, so I could experience his presence more deeply in Israel and who inspired me to create this book.

References

[1] Calvin, John (1509-1564). Theologian, pastor and reformer.

[2] Ignatius of Loyola (1491-1556). Fleming, David, SJ (2011) *Draw me Into Your Friendship: The Spiritual Exercises*. Saint Louis, Missouri. The Institute of Jesuit Sources.

[3] Richard Rohr, Leader of Center for Action and Contemplation, priest, and author.

[4] Fleisher, Sheryl, Spiritual Director. *Joy,* Unpublished. Used with permission.

About the Author

Anne is an author, Spiritual Director, and workshop presenter who lives with her husband in San Diego. She published her first book *Not Alone: A Christ-Centered Recovery Process for Women who have Experienced Physical, Emotional or Sexual Trauma* (2019) and her second book *Not Alone: Transforming Trauma and Accompanying Survivors (2020)* after her own healing experience and leading trauma groups for women. She has also published several articles for magazines on how to accompany survivors of trauma for spiritual directors, clergy, and family members.

Visit her website at annemarierichardson.com.

Made in the USA
Columbia, SC
25 January 2021